# The Origin a
# an Old Masonic Lodge

"The Caveac", no. 176 of ancient
free & accepted masons of England

John Percy Simpson

Alpha Editions

This edition published in 2019

ISBN : 9789353951009

Design and Setting By
**Alpha Editions**
email - alphaedis@gmail.com

As per information held with us this book is in Public Domain. This book is a reproduction of an important historical work. Alpha Editions uses the best technology to reproduce historical work in the same manner it was first published to preserve its original nature. Any marks or number seen are left intentionally to preserve its true form.

# The Origin and History

OF AN

## OLD MASONIC LODGE,

# "THE CAVEAC,"

### No. 176.

OF

### Ancient Free & Accepted Masons of England

(*ILLUSTRATED*),

BY

JOHN PERCY SIMPSON, P.M. & P.Z.

---

"Footprints on the sands of Time."—*Longfellow.*

To

The Worshipful Master,

The Wardens, and Brethren

of the

Caveac Lodge, No. 176,

This little Volume is

Respectfully and Fraternally dedicated.

# LIST OF ILLUSTRATIONS.

|  | PAGE. |
|---|---|
| THE LATE DR. CHARLES BROWNE, P.M. & D.C. (1868-1905) (AS MASTER OF THE SOCIETY OF APOTHECARIES) ... | *Frontispiece* |
| THE LATE REV. R. J. SIMPSON, M.A., P.G.C., CHAPLAIN OF THE LODGE FROM 1885 TO 1900 | 4 |
| THE CHURCH OF ST. BENNET FINCK, THREADNEEDLE STREET, IN 1811 | 11 |
| PERCIVAL ALLEYNE NAIRNE, P.M., P.G.D. (TREASURER FROM 1877 TO 1881, AND FROM 1885 TO 1904) | 17 |
| FROM "STOW'S SURVEY OF BROAD STREET WARD, 1750" ... | 21 |
| HOUSES IN SPREAD EAGLE COURT FORMING THE OLD CAVEAC TAVERN, FROM A PICTURE OF 1800 ... | 33 |
| THE LATE GEORGE KEENE LEMANN, MASTER, 1873 ... | 35 |
| VIEW OF HAMMERSMITH FROM CHISWICK, ABOUT 1770... | 39 |
| "WINDSOR CASTLE INN," HAMMERSMITH (PRESENT DAY) ... | 43 |
| JOHN SICH, P.M., BREWER, CHISWICK. (INITIATED 1774, DIED 1836. A MEMBER OF THE LODGE FOR 62 YEARS)... | 51 |
| DUKE OF SUSSEX, GRAND MASTER (1813-1843) ... | 57 |
| OLD TYLER'S SWORD, PRESENTED BY THOMAS BROWN IN 1787 | 61 |
| ELIJAH LITCHFIELD, P.M., SECRETARY FROM 1852 TO 1875 ... | 65 |
| CHARLES DOREY, P.M., SECRETARY FROM 1875 TO 1889 ... | 66 |
| OLD LOVING CUP, PRESENTED BY THE REV. R. J. SIMPSON, P.G.C., IN 1887 | 69 |
| PAST MASTER'S JEWEL AND CENTENARY JEWEL OF CAVEAC LODGE, NO. 176 ... | 75 |

# CONTENTS.

|  | PAGE |
|---|---|
| PREFACE ... ... ... ... ... ... ... ... | 1—2 |
| INTRODUCTORY ... ... ... ... ... ... ... | 5 |
| CHAPTER I.—HOW DID THE LODGE COME TO BE CALLED THE CAVEAC LODGE? ... ... ... ... ... | 6—15 |
| CHAPTER II.—WHAT IS THE ORIGIN OF THE WORD CAVEAC ITSELF, AND FROM WHOM WAS IT DERIVED? | 16—29 |
| CHAPTER III.—THE LATER HISTORY OF THE "CAVEAC TAVERN" ... ... ... ... ... ... | 30—37 |
| CHAPTER IV.—HISTORY OF THE CAVEAC LODGE SINCE 1768 | 38—76 |
| APPENDIX ... ... ... ... ... ... ... ... | 77—84 |
| GENERAL INDEX ... ... ... ... ... ... ... | 85—89 |

## PREFACE.

Dear Brethren,

I am sure you will understand me when I say that the writing of this little History of our dear old Lodge has afforded me nothing but pleasure, and interest, and if in reading it you derive even the smallest portion of that pleasure, and interest I am indeed amply rewarded.

I decided to write this short preface because I well know that there are several old Members of our Lodge much better qualified in every respect to compile such a History, and I want to make it quite clear that it was not premeditated design, or deep preliminary research that led me to commence this paper, but pure accident. What an interesting volume could be made out of the "accidents" that have led persons to begin literary works, the inception of which would never have occurred to them otherwise !

In this case the accident was a curious one. As First Principal of the Caveac Chapter I had the privilege of exalting our Brother Colonel Green Thompson of the Caveac Lodge. I had ascertained when making some researches into the History of Royal Arch Masonry that the fourth actual Warrant granted to a Chapter was conferred on the Chapter of the Royal Inniskilling Dragoons at York, and dated 3rd October, 1770. In proposing the health of our Companion at the Banquet I mentioned this fact as interesting to one who had lately commanded this Regiment. Companion Green Thompson asked me afterwards to obtain if possible some further facts relating to the Masonic traditions of the Regiment, as he was shortly dining with their Colonel-in-Chief, His Royal Highness the Duke of Connaught, and would like to be in a position to refer to the matter. I promised to do so and of course visited the Grand Lodge Library. There, with the kind aid of Brother Sadler, some facts of interest were gathered together. Looking through one of the Indexes for the word "Cavalry" I came across the word "Caveac." I thought naturally that it referred to our present Lodge, but on looking further I found that I had got the wrong index, and this one related to ancient meeting places of Masonic Lodges. Thereupon followed further researches, the results of which are embodied in this little Book.

I here take the opportunity of thanking W. Bro. P. A. Nairne, P.G.D., our worthy Treasurer, W. Bro. Mihill Slaughter, P.M., P.A.G.D.C., Bro. White, P.M., Bro. Matveieff, P.M., and Bro. R. Davies, P.M. for their kind assistance.

Yours fraternally,

J. P. SIMPSON,

P.M., P.Z. 176.

4, NEW COURT,
LINCOLN'S INN, W.C.

REVD R. J. SIMPSON, P.G.C.
CHAPLAIN 1885 TO 1900.

# THE ORIGIN AND HISTORY

OF

# AN OLD MASONIC LODGE, "THE CAVEAC," No. 176.

THE Warrant of this old Masonic Lodge known as the "Caveac Lodge" is dated the 21st May, 1768, and it has since 1874 held its meetings at the Albion Tavern, Aldersgate Street.

It has always been a matter of conjecture as to why the somewhat curious name "Caveac" was adopted by this Lodge, and what was the derivation and meaning of the word itself. Some have thought that it was a corruption of the word "Caveat," and others that it referred to some person or place. In looking through modern directories however no person or place can apparently at the present day claim this word.

I think that by enquiries in various quarters I am now able to throw some light upon this vexed question. I need scarcely say that in my researches at the Grand Lodge Library I received the ever able, and courteous assistance of Brother Henry Sadler, Grand Tyler and Sub-Librarian.

The Origin and History of the Lodge may be conveniently considered under four heads; (1) How did the Lodge come to be called the "Caveac Lodge"? (2) What is the origin of the word "Caveac" itself, and from whom was it derived? (3) The later History of "The Caveac Tavern"; (4) History of the Caveac Lodge since 1768.

## CHAPTER I

### How did the Lodge come to be called the Caveac Lodge?

IT will be within your knowledge that the Grand Lodge was first constituted in 1717. About 1751 a number of lodges in London mostly composed of Irish Masons formed themselves into a separate body. Those that supported the Grand Lodge of 1717 were generally denominated "Moderns" to distinguish them from the other party who styled themselves "Antients."

I now find among the "Modern" Lodges was a Lodge No. 86 in the Constitution of 1736, and meeting at the "Caveac Tavern," Spread Eagle Court, Finch Lane, in the Parish of St. Bennet Finck, in the City of London. It was a "Master's Lodge," that is to say it had the authority of Grand Lodge to confer the Higher Degrees.

The neighbourhood was not without its Masonic memories and associations as the first recorded Grand Lodge of England was held in the Merchant Taylors' Hall, just east of Finch Lane, on the 24th June, 1723. The Duke of Wharton presiding as Grand Master, and the Rev. J. T. Desaguliers, LL.D., acting as Deputy Grand Master. The Duke of Norfolk was also Installed Grand Master at the Merchant Taylors' Hall on the 29th January, 1730.

In the Grand Lodge Minutes, 19th December, 1729, we find that a lodge was meeting at that date at the Three Tuns, Swithin's Alley, close by. This is now the Old Dundee

Lodge, No. 18. Another lodge was meeting at the Swan and Rummer, Finch Lane, now the Castle Lodge of Harmony, No. 26.

It was one of the faults of the "Moderns" that they were negligent in returning their Lists of Members to Grand Lodge, and most unfortunately we have no return by the Lodge meeting at the Caveac Tavern It was however meeting at the Tavern from 1755 to 1768 on the 2nd and 4th Wednesdays in every month. We know only that the Treasurer of the Lodge was named Wm. Acton. This brother was Master in April, 1767, and the last Master of the Lodge as then constituted.

As Brother Acton's name is the only one we can find as officially associated with the Lodge at the Caveac Tavern I thought it would be interesting, if possible, to obtain some facts as to his identity and career. After some trouble I found in the Broad Street Ward Minutes (Manuscript 1228 in the Guildhall Library) of the 22nd December, 1762, that William Acton was on that date elected Treasurer of the Ward, and in 1771 he was elected as Common Councillor. He died early in 1782, but later on, in 1792, we see the name of another William Acton, no doubt his son. St. Bennet Finck was in the Ward of Broad Street, but William Acton is described as of St. Margaret's Lothbury. Brother Acton's will is dated 2nd November, 1781. He is there described as a "Painter." The Will deals with a considerable amount of money, and appoints his son William Acton executor, but does not present any interesting features except perhaps one. He leaves all his rights and interest in the "Contumvirate Society, now held at the King's Head Tavern, Poultry," to his son. What was the Contumvirate Society ? My enquiries have entirely failed to answer the query.

At the time Bro. Acton was elected Treasurer of the Ward, a Mr. Thomas Rawlinson was Alderman, afterwards Lord Mayor, and knighted in 1753. He appears to have been the son of Sir Thomas Rawlinson, Lord Mayor in 1706, and therefore a brother of Dr. Richard Rawlinson, the distinguished Masonic Historian, and Antiquarian, who died in 1755. (Gould's History, Vol. II. p. 169). I cannot find that the Alderman was himself a Mason.

In the Grand Lodge records we see that on the 17th October, 1766, 21s. was paid by the Lodge to Charity, and three Members of the Lodge attended at Grand Lodge on that occasion, and on the 15th April, 1767, a like sum was paid and two members attended. Opposite to the name of the Lodge in the Engraved Lists for 1768 is this entry " no Lodge meeting here." There is no evidence of actual erasure of the Lodge which would only be done in the case of contumnacy. Nor would there be a return of the Warrant as at that time the Minutes of the first or Consecration Meeting, signed by the Grand Officers attending, or in the country by duly deputed Brethren, formed the Warrant for working.

Now, before entering on the question of the establishment of the present Caveac Lodge at Hammersmith, I wish to touch upon a matter which I consider in some measure explains and supports the theory I shall later on put forward.

If we examine contemporary writers at the time of the great Plague and Fire of London in 1666 and 1667, such as the Diaries of Pepys and Evelyn, and the narrative of Defoe, we learn that a vast number of the inhabitants of the City of London migrated to the country villages as they then were in the vicinity.

It is interesting to note that Defoe himself lived in 1702 in Freeman's Court, Cornhill, almost adjoining Spread Eagle

Court, and doubtless visited the Caveac Tavern where he would have found congenial company. There is a proclamation describing him as of this Court, dated the 10th January, 1702, ordering his arrest for writing a pamphlet entitled "The shortest way with Dissenters." Defoe was buried in Bunhill Fields, 26th April, 1731, as " Mr. Dubow, from St. Gile's, Cripplegate." A curious instance of the eccentric spelling of those days to which later I shall call attention.

A great many of those who so migrated no doubt returned to reside again in or near their old homes, but a considerable minority of merchants and tradesmen had found from experience that they could live in the country, and yet carry on their business in the City.

The roads also at the end of the 17th century, apart from the great highways, began to improve, and the first Act for the repair of the Public Roads was passed in 1698. Without doubt, the early part of the 18th century saw a marked advance in the security, and facilities for travel to and from the City. In Kent's Guide to London 1740, we note that two coaches started daily for Hammersmith from the Chequer's Ale House, Chequer's Court, Charing Cross, and two from the Golden Cross for Hampton Court *via* Hammersmith and Twickenham. Later in the century they ran about every two hours, mostly starting from Piccadilly.

The citizens of London in the 18th century appear to have resided either in the City itself or in the Suburbs, and not in the West End of London. Indeed there was no period perhaps when the separation of the Aristocracy of the West, and the Traders of the East was more distinct and clearly defined. On rare occasions only the upper classes invaded the City, as in the case of the South Sea Bubble. Thus we see that a number of residences were erected about the beginning of the 18th century in Stepney, Bethnal Green, Tottenham, and Islington, and even further afield in Hackney and Hampstead to the north, Kensington and Hammersmith to the West, and Kennington and Dulwich to the South. So the country villages of the 17th century began to be more intimately connected with, and drawn into the life of the City, and the suburban system gradually developed.

With regard to the particular locality in which we are interested, namely, Finch Lane—or Finck Lane as it was originally called after the family of Finck who owned most of the property in the neighbourhood in the 17th century—it was entirely burnt down in 1666, and the old Parish Church of St. Bennet Finck, built in 1633 by Robert Finck the Elder, also perished. The church was rebuilt from a design of Sir Christopher Wren, and of this church as it stood in 1811 I have fortunately obtained a rare print, drawn and etched by J. Wedgwood. Under the Royal Exchange Rebuilding Act, 1838, the church was pulled down, and the various blocks of buildings between the Exchange, and Finch Lane, including the old Spread Eagle Court, gradually disappeared between the years 1840 and 1850. Threadneedle Street (in the early Surveys called Three-needle Street) was widened considerably, and modern offices and chambers built as we see them for the most part at the present time.

In comparison with the Great Fire of 1666 one hears but little of the two terrible fires that devastated the City on March 25th, 1748, and November 7th, 1765. The first commenced in a barber's shop in Change Alley, and an interesting account of this Fire can be read in the London Magazine for March, 1748, vol. xvii., p. 139. The second, curiously enough, began in another barber's shop at the corner where Bishopsgate Street joins Leadenhall Street. In both cases whole rows of shops, houses, and taverns were burnt down.

VIEW OF CHURCH OF ST. BENNET FINCK.

The fire in 1765 was perhaps the most disastrous as the whole of Bishopsgate Street was consumed, and a large portion of Threadneedle Street and Cornhill, but it reached no further west towards Finch Lane than the Merchant Taylors' Hall, which was seriously damaged. About eleven Taverns and Coffee houses were destroyed, amongst others the famous White Lion Tavern, Bishopsgate Street, and the Bull Inn, Leadenhall Street. R. Wilkinson in his " Londinia," giving an account of this Fire, points out that all the tradesmen and inhabitants were dispersed in various parts of London and the suburbs, and that many never returned. He emphasises this by quoting from the notices of removal in the " Public Ledger " and other journals of the time.

As I have mentioned, the Warrant of the Lodge meeting at the " Windsor Castle," Hammersmith, is dated the 21st May, 1768, I purposely do not call it the " Caveac Lodge," as Lane in his List of Lodges at anyrate says that the name was not adopted till 1778. I doubt whether this, however, is correct, as the first returns to Grand Lodge are headed " Caveac Lodge," and the Warrant is endorsed with this name. It received the Number 424, and this has been altered on no less than seven occasions, as will be seen by reference to the Appendix. In the body of the Warrant *(see Appendix I.)* three Brethren are mentioned, namely, John Maddocks, Master ; Henry Adams, S.W. ; and Vaughan, J.W. ; and to these Brethren I shall have occasion to refer again later on. It is curious that in the first return to Grand Lodge their names are not mentioned amongst the Founders, a list of whose names will be found in Chapter IV. None of the names of these Brethren appear in the Lists of Lodges returned to Grand Lodge prior to 1768, though all were, of course, Masons. It is important to note also that there was no Lodge in the neighbourhood of

Hammersmith prior to 1768. I observe the name of a John Wilson amongst the Ratepayers of St. Bennet Finck, and it disappears in 1760; but the name is a very common one, and there is nothing to identify him with the Founder in the above list, who is therein described as a Vintner.

For the reasons I have mentioned above suburban life was slowly and gradually developing during the early part of the 18th century, and later Masonry had in like manner began to extend its influence in various directions. We find, for instance, St. George's Lodge, No. 140, and St. Luke's Lodge, No. 144, consecrated at Chelsea about 1765, the Lodge of St. Faith at Woolwich, St. Peter's Lodge at Southwark, and the Castle Lodge at Putney. The Bank of England Lodge removed to Bermondsey at a little later date.

My theory is that some of the original members of the Lodge of Hammersmith, and those who joined it shortly after its foundation, were Members of the old Lodge meeting at the Caveac Tavern, and when a name came to be chosen, selected that of their old meeting place in the City, a place to which, possibly in the daytime, some still occasionally resorted. In 1768 a number of Lodges of course had no distinct names, being known as Lodges meeting at the " Blue Post," " Black Bull," &c. About this period, however, they began to adopt names often signifying Masonic virtues, such as " Harmony," " Concord," " Honour," but many selected the names of places of meeting or localities, such as " King's Arms," " Westminster and Keystone," &c. Perhaps the best instance of this form of adoption for our purpose is mentioned in Brother Sadler's most interesting " Memorials of the Globe Lodge," page 7. This old Lodge met at the Globe Tavern, Fleet Street, in 1764, and shortly afterwards selected the name of its meeting place, and has ever since been known as " The Globe Lodge."

The dates I have quoted are of course very significant, the Lodge meeting at the Caveac Tavern ceased to meet there in 1768, and the Lodge at Hammersmith, known as the "Caveac Lodge," commenced its meetings in that year, and further, I think, there was some connection between the Caveac Tavern, and the Windsor Castle.

## CHAPTER II.

### WHAT IS THE ORIGIN OF THE WORD "CAVEAC" ITSELF, AND HOW WAS IT DERIVED?

IN the earlier engraved Lists of Lodges and their meeting places in the Grand Lodge Library the first column gives the sign of the Tavern such as a Globe, Bell, or Sun. In the case of the Caveac Tavern none is given, the inference therefore is that it was the personal name of the original proprietor.

The Licensing Records of the City do not go back beyond 1840, and the Church of St. Bennet Finck was, as mentioned above, also pulled down about that time, and the Parish incorporated with St. Peter le Poer, Broad Street. Some however of the old Parish Records have been happily preserved in the vaults of the Guildhall Library, and the registers are in the Church of St. Peter le Poer. Amongst the records are the Vestry Minutes from 1660, and the Churchwardens' Accounts from about the same time to 1828. These are numbered 1303 and 1304 in the Manuscript Catalogue of the Library.

In the Churchwardens' Accounts and Lists of Parishioners assessed we find in 1687 the first mention of a Mr. Bertrand Cahuac. He was probably a young man at that time about 25, and his name, I think, implies that he was a Frenchman, a native of Languedoc, where the names

P. A. NAIRNE, P.M., P.G.D.
Treasurer 1877 to 1881 and 1885 to 1904.

commonly end in "ac" or "oc," *e.g.*, Cognac, Barsac, Panillac, and Pontac. I cannot find, however, any trace of a family of this name in France, the nearest approach to it being the family name of "Cahusac." A prominent member of this family, Louis de Cahusac, flourished about 1745 as a writer of plays, and died in Paris 1759.

There had been a considerable influx of Frenchmen into England during the reigns of Charles II. and James II., many of whom had connections attached to the Court.

A number of French names are to be noted in the Parish of St. Bennet Finck, and the immediate neighbourhood. Possibly they were attracted to the locality after the Revocation of the Edict of Nantes by the Walloon or Protestant French Church, which stood at the north side of Threadneedle Street, opposite the end of Finch Lane (see Stow's Survey, 1750). This Church was built in the reign of Elizabeth, destroyed in the great Fire, afterwards restored and finally pulled down in 1830. The Église Protestants Francaise de Londres, the successor of the said Church, now stands in Soho Square, and I had the pleasure of an interview with its courteous Pastor M. Degremont, B.A., who allowed me to inspect the old books and registers.

It would seem that Bertrand Cahuac set up as a wine seller in Spread Eagle Court, Finch Lane. He may have been assisted in this by an elder brother, who, I fancy, must then have been living in England. Doubtless he prospered, as his assessment gradually increased until in his latter years he was the chief contributor to the Rates, and was assessed in respect of four houses. In Stow's "Survey of London, 1750," we see a block of four houses on the west side of Spread Eagle Court, reaching up to and facing Threadneedle Street, and some six on the east; and we find from the

Parish books that Mr. Cahuac's houses and Tavern formed the block to the west.

The situation of the houses next to the church is fairly indicated by the following extract from the Vestry Minutes, dated the 16th October, 1729. "Agreed that Mr. Cahuac have the liberty of making a leaden pipe to convey the water from the top of his houses and over to the vestry leads, he paying 1s. and to repair all damages that may be sustained by breaking of said pipe."

It is curious to note how the spelling of Mr. Bertrand's surname gradually became corrupted, or perhaps I had better say Anglicised. I find in the Churchwarden's lists first "Cahuac" then "Cavehac," and later from about 1710, generally "Caveac."

In the list of offices served by the principal inhabitants at the end of Vestry Minutes, vol. ii., we have it plainly written "Bert Caveac." Nearly all the references to the Tavern are also spelt in this way, or with an extra "k" on the end. For instance, we find in the Churchwarden's Accounts, 1758, " For the Knell Bell for Mr. Fisher, cook at Caveack's Tavern, 5s." In the next item a Mr. Holloway or his representatives are charged 10s. for tolling the "Great Bell" after his decease.

One of the later references in the Vestry Minutes, however, reverts to the original spelling of the name. It is as follows :—

"14th April, 1747. The Committee appointed 19th "August last, met at Cahuac's and their unanimous "decision was that such part of the houses of Thomas "Sergison now known by the names of the 'Three Tuns "Tavern,' 'The Bluecoat,' and 'Chadwell's Coffee "House,' as shewn on the freehold belonging to the "Parish, is near one-third the value of the whole, and

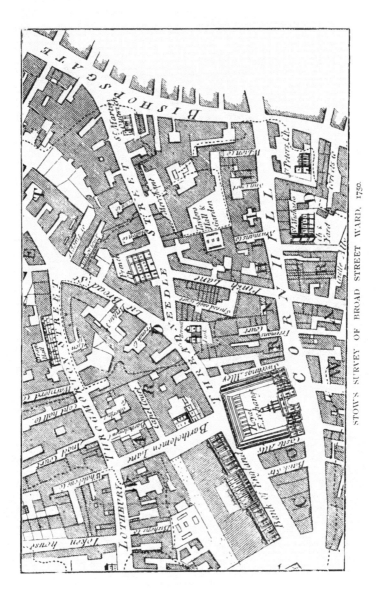

STOW'S SURVEY OF BROAD STREET WARD, 1750.

"that on the said Sergison surrendering the old lease
"and paying a fine of £100 for the use of the poor we
"recommend the grant of a new lease for 99 years at
" £20 per annum."

In the accounts also of 1764 we have these two entries :—

"30th June, 1764. Paid at Cahuac's, about Lecturer,
" £1 9s. 0d."

"10th December, 1764. Paid at Cahuac's, about
"Jetty, £2 7s. 6d."

The Parish meetings at this period appear to have been always held here, and refreshment followed labour.

The "Lecturer" above-mentioned refers to a small charitable trust for providing an assistant clergyman to preach at the evening service. The "Jetty" seems to have been a sad bone of contention between the Parish of St. Bennet Finck, and the adjoining Parish to the west. It consisted of some overhanging buildings in Sweeting's Rents, facing the Royal Exchange. The foundations being in one Parish, and the upper stories in the other. This delicate question required frequent meetings at the Caveac Tavern.

While on the Vestry Minutes, I may mention that on the 13th December, 1750, a certain prominent parishioner named Robert Crucefex was elected Churchwarden, and on his refusing to serve was fined £2. The name is rare. Could this be the grandfather or father of our distinguished Brother, Dr. Robert Crucefex, P.G.D., and the Founder of the Asylum for aged Freemasons? Bro. Crucefex was, I see, educated at the Merchant Taylors' School.

In 1704 Mr. Bert. Caveac served the office of Constable to the Parish, and in the Vestry Minutes of 16th December, 1704, he was chosen Questioner and Churchwarden in rotation. Apparently, however, he refused to serve, as we next find this entry : "agreed that Mr. Bert Cahuac was admitted to a fine of £14 for offices by him unserved." This is a large sum for those times and is, in fact, the largest fine imposed in these Minutes on any parishioner. I gather also that it was only in the later period of Mr. Bertrand's occupancy of the Tavern that the Vestry went there for wine or refreshments, although it was next door to the church. From these facts and other slight indications I presume our friend was not in his early days very acceptable to the Church, and State as then constituted. Those were stirring times. James II. had just died in exile, and another ten years saw the landing of the Pretender. Was this foreigner and keeper of a tavern, the resort of one or more Masonic Lodges, a Jacobite? Of course, it is not the place here to enter upon the most interesting question as to whether in the beginning of the 18th century Masons as a body inclined to the Stuart faction. Personally, I think, such evidence as remains to us shows that at anyrate the Scotch and Irish Masons did, but that later the interest shewn in Masonry by the reigning Family, the establishment of many Military Lodges, and other causes, gradually dispelled any such political bias.

Mr. Bertrand Cahuac, or Caveac, carried on the Tavern till 1738, when he retired. I think that prior to this an elder brother of Bertrand had resided at the little village of Beddington, near Croydon. There at any rate lived in 1738 his two nephews, John and James, and to this retired spot the old man went to pass his last days. I call him an old man, because if we assume that he was 25 when he first appears in the Parish Lists of St. Bennet Finck in 1687, he was, at any rate in 1738, aged 76, and probably he was really some years older.

He made his Will on the 2nd August, 1741, and died at Beddington on the 8th of April, 1743. The entry in the Parish Register of Burials as shown by the Certificate is as follows:

"1743, Bertrand Cahuac, April 14th, Registered Affidavit April 14th." The Testator's Will was duly proved by his Executor and nephew John Cahuac, and I have obtained a copy of the Will from the Prerogative Wills at Somerset House. It is short, and I think it more satisfactory to set it out at length.

EXTRACTED FROM THE PRINCIPAL REGISTRY OF THE PROBATE DIVORCE AND ADMIRALTY DIVISION OF THE HIGH COURT OF JUSTICE IN THE PREROGATIVE COURT OF CANTERBURY.

IN THE NAME OF GOD AMEN WHEREAS I, BERTRAND CAHUAC of Beddington in the County of Surry Gentleman have made one or more wills and codicils and thereby or by one of them gave among other things unto my nephew James Cahuac the sum of two hundred pounds and unto my nephew James Chammont the sum of Fifty pounds and having lately engaged my executors to pay unto Martha Cahuac the sum of two hundred pounds for and towards discharging a debt due from my said nephew James Cahuac unto the estate of the said Zachary Cahuac and also the further sum of fifty pounds for and towards discharging a debt due from my said nephew James Chammont unto the estate of my said nephew Zachary Cahuac and several persons being dead since I made my former wills and other circumstances intervening inducing me to revoke all former wills and make a new one I do accordingly hereby revoke all former wills by me at any time heretofore made and declare this only to be and contain my last will and testament in manner as follows And first I do direct my executor hereafter named to bury me decently in the churchyard of Beddington aforesaid in a vault to be dugg and made for that purpose (if the parish will so permit it) about eight or ten foot from the wall and about four foot deep over which I would have a black marble stone and iron railes round it and if the parson and major part of the parishioners having power so to do will on request meet and assign the ground for the purpose aforesaid and appropriate it as a burying place for me and my family Then I give unto the Church Wardens of Beddington the sum of twenty pounds to be applied for the use of the poor of that parish and in case the parish will not sett apart such piece of ground for a burying place as aforesaid then I would be buried in such place and manner as my executor shall think fit item in case my said nephew James Cahuac shall pay what he owes unto the estate of my said late nephew Zachary Cahuac whereby my executor will be discharged from the payment of the said two hundred pounds  Then I give and devise unto my said nephew James Cahuac that sum of two hundred pounds to be paid him in six months next after my decease  And in case my said nephew James Chammont shall also pay what he owes unto the said estate of my said nephew Zachary Cahuac whereby my executor will all be discharged from the payment of the said fifty pounds  Then I also give unto my said nephew James Chammont that sum of fifty pounds to be paid him in such time as aforesaid  Item I direct my executor to lay out ten pounds in some piece of plate which I give to my Godson Bertrand Cahuac to keep in memory of me  And lastly as to all other my real and personal estate whatsoever and wheresoever I give and devise the same unto my nephew John Cahuac his heirs and assigns for ever and appoint him sole EXECUTOR of this my will contained in this one sheet of paper  IN WITNESS whereof I have hereunto set my hand and seal this twenty second day of August in the year of our Lord one thousand seven hundred and forty one—The mark of BERTRAND

CAHUAC SIGNED sealed published and declared by the said testator as his last will and testament in the presence of us who have subscribed our names hereto in his presence and at his request FRANCIS ABRAHM LeCONTE—PET T. ELOY—JOHN HOWARD.

Proved 11th April 1743.

The witnesses to the will are Francis Abraham Le Conte, Peter T. Eloy, and John Howard. We may consider it certain that the last named witness, John Howard, was the "John Howard" whose name appears in the Parish Lists of St. Bennet Finck, as a very near neighbour of Cahuac's, for many years in Spread Eagle Court. The Howard family were well known in the Parish, and I shall have to refer again to them later on. The name also of "Le Conte" appears on several occasions from 1700 onwards in the old registers of the French Protestant Church, Threadneedle Street.

There are two other entries in the Beddington Registers not far removed in date which are interesting to us, and the certificates give, at the same time, instances of the modern spelling of the name. They are :—

"Birth, 1738—Martha, daughter of John and Sarah "Caveac, 1738—February 28th."

"Birth, 1741—Bertrand, son of John and Sarah "Caveac, April 29th."

This Bertrand was no doubt the Godson mentioned in the will to whom he bequeaths a piece of plate.

There can be no doubt that Bertrand Cahuac was buried in the beautiful churchyard of Beddington, but after long search no trace of his tombstone could be found. The old sexton—who had been there over 30 years—assisted me, and showed me a tombstone which appeared to bear the date 1743, and answered to the description in the will, and he believed it to be the one, but unfortunately, with every wish to recognise the name, I could not honestly do so. The sexton informed me that the late Rector, Canon Bridges, used to go round with the old burial registers, and with hammer and chisel himself renew the inscriptions. If he had been alive the sexton thought the old Rector would have been able to point the grave out to me ; but alas ! this second "Old Mortality" died some ten years ago.

As far as my researches go there is only one entry in the Parish registers of St. Bennet Finck in relation to this family. We have the following "Ann Caveac, daughter of James and Ann, his wife, born 14th January, 1732." This no doubt is the other nephew mentioned in the will who was perhaps then residing with his uncle. We hear no more of James, but John Caveac appears by the Parish Lists to have come and resided in his uncle's old Parish in 1769, and died there in 1781.

It is interesting to note that James Watt, the Scotch engineer and inventor of steam locomotion, was, for some time, about 1765, working for John Morgan, an instrument maker at the corner of Finch Lane, a few yards from the Caveac Tavern.

Malcolm in his "Londinium Redivivum," 1802, mentions that at that time there was a marble tablet on the south wall of St. Bennet Finck to the memory of "Mr. Timothy Helmesley, citizen and mercer, Common Councillor of Broad Street Ward. He lived respected and died regretted, 1765, aged 72 years."

He was Common Councillor with Bro. Acton, master of the Caveac Lodge in 1767, and he lived in Spread Eagle Court opposite the Caveac Tavern from 1734. This colleague of Bro. Acton's was also a prominent member of the Vestry of St. Bennet Finck from about 1740 up to his death. Was he also a Master of the old Caveac Lodge ?

I have mentioned that the lodge meetings at the Caveac Tavern were held on the 2nd and 4th Wednesdays in every month. I find also after some careful examination that at anyrate some of the vestry meetings to which I have alluded above were also held on these days. Is this a coincidence, or may it not well be that some of the members of the vestry were members of the Lodge also, and the meetings were arranged to fit in? The vestry meeting would perhaps be held about 4 o'clock. There was not generally an excess of business, and then at the end of the Minutes we find invariably the words "Adjourned to Caveac's." Dinner would be served about 5 o'clock, when Bro. Acton, and the other brethren from the neighbouring Parishes would drop in, dressed in their square cut brown cloth coats, and spotless linen. Afterwards the lodge is held, and then a pleasant social evening is spent in the old Tavern with churchwarden pipes, and cheered by a glass or two of punch served by the worthy landlady, with the appropriate name of Bowles. The failings, and fallings away of the "Antients" are discussed, local politics are fought over again, the "jetty" the "lecturer," and "Wilkes and Liberty," varied perchance with an argument as to Garrick's last play, Goldsmith's last poem, or Johnson's last saying.

It is indeed pleasant to picture and revive the past, though the actors be but shadows on a stage long vanished and forgotten.

## CHAPTER III.

#### THE LATER HISTORY OF "THE CAVEAC TAVERN."

AFTER Bertrand had retired, in 1738, the four houses in respect of which he was assessed are transferred into the name of "Zackariah Caveac," in one entry described as a widow. There is no evidence to show that this lady was the wife of Bertrand, indeed, if she had been, the probabilities are he would have mentioned her in his will. He does mention as we have seen a nephew "Zackary," possibly this was the mother or sister of this nephew. The name of Zackariah Caveac disappears in 1741, and she is succeeded by a Mr. Bowler Miller. He is succeeded in 1752 by Judith Jones, and in 1757 a Mrs. Ann Bowles appears on the scene. She was the hostess during most of the time our Brethren frequented the Caveac, and I fancy the Tavern was during her time very prosperous. The Vestry, as I have mentioned, often held their meetings and dined there, and there are further numerous items in the Churchwardens' accounts of "Mrs. Ann Bowles, for wine supplied." A rather celebrated Divine was then Rector of St. Bennet Finck, the Rev. Dr. Waterland, a popular preacher, and well known throughout the City.

It is rather a curious coincidence that Mrs. Bowles' occupancy of the tavern ended in 1768, the same year that the lodge was formed at Hammersmith, but in the next Chapter I shall put forward a possible theory as to where she removed.

For reasons that will be apparent hereafter it is material to note carefully her successors in the premises, as shown by the Parish Records—

| | | | | | |
|---|---|---|---|---|---|
| Thomas Clark | held the premises from | | | | 1768 to 1774 |
| John Edis | ,, | ,, | ,, | ,, | 1774 to 1804 |
| Mary Edis (widow) | ,, | ,, | ,, | ,, | 1804 to 1810 |
| Thomas Crow | ,, | ,, | ,, | ,, | 1810 to 1827 |
| Alexander Cooper | ,, | ,, | ,, | ,, | 1827 to 1831 |
| Alexander Cooper and Thomas Walker Cooper | ,, | ,, | ,, | ,, | 1831 to 1848 |

The houses were all pulled down about 1849.

The Thomas Clark above-mentioned is probably the Thomas Clark who is known to have lived in this neighbourhood about this date, and afterwards migrated to the Strand, where he was called the "King of Exeter Exchange." He died in 1816 worth half-a-million sterling.

In 1774 John Edis was elected "Upper Butler" to the Ward of Broad Street.

In the year 1795 the name of Michael Lemann appears for the first time next door to John Edis, and he took some of the premises which had formerly formed part of the Caveac Tavern, and set up a Biscuit Manufactory. On the other side of Mr. Crow later appears the name of Mr. Bannister, Butcher.

Now, in 1895, a Mr. Callow published an interesting book entitled, "Old London Taverns." In the preface he sets out the reasons that induced him to write the book. It appears that George Augustus Sala had written a letter to the *Daily Telegraph* in which he had mentioned that in his early days at "Joe's Coffee House" in Finch Lane, you could have your own meat cooked for lunch. Thereupon Callow wrote a letter to the *Pall Mall Gazette* to contradict this statement, pointing out that the custom referred to by Sala did exist, but that he had mistaken the house. That he (Callow) was accustomed in the early Forties to buy a chop or steak at Bannister's the butcher and take it to " The Spread Eagle " next door, where they cooked it.

This dispute suggested to Mr. Callow the writing of " Old London Taverns." In its preface he quotes the letter to the *Pall Mall*, and in a note points out that he was mistaken in the name " Spread Eagle," the house being known as the " Fleece and Sun," Spread Eagle Court. He described it as standing between Bannister's and Lemann's. " A public house of the old City type, with its dining room fitted with boxes as still to be seen at the " Cheshire Cheese " and some other places in the by-streets of the City, with a sanded floor." And later on in the body of the book, page 30, he says, " Opposite to where the Telegraph Office now stands between " the North British Life Office, and the Hercules Passage " entrance to the Stock Exchange, once stood the " Old Fleece " and Sun Tavern," kept by two brothers named Cooper, at the " corner of Spread Eagle Court, a narrow passage then leading " into Finch Lane. Customers used to select their chops and " steaks at Bannister's, and then went into the " Fleece & Sun," " and handed it over to the cook or waiter with instructions. " The charge was 3d. for " bread, cooking and 'taters." " Decorations or embellishments there were none, but though " the place looked rough it was scrupulously clean."

The wines drunk were mostly port and sherry.

There is an engraving on page 31 in Callow's History of Lemann's standing alone, with the houses on either side already demolished.

VIEW OF HOUSES IN SPREAD EAGLE COURT,
FORMING THE OLD CAVEAC LODGE (1800).

I think there is not the slightest doubt that the "Caveac Tavern" and the "Fleece and Sun" were one and the same house, the latter however forming only a portion of the premises held by Caveac. The exact period when the name was changed is not easy to determine. There is clear

GEORGE KEENE LEMANN, P.M. (1873).

evidence to show that up to 1795 the Tavern was a considerable Inn, including most of the premises then taken by Lemann, and that the outhouses, and probably rooms for Masonic gatherings, &c., stretched far back into the Spread Eagle Court behind,

Through the kindness of Messrs. Drew & Co., the present owners of Messrs. Lemann's business, I have been able to obtain a photograph of a picture painted about 1800, showing Lemann's premises, and the "Fleece and Sun" as they then stood. The houses are described as of Threadneedle Street, but as a matter of fact, in all the Parish records they then, and until they were pulled down, formed part of Spread Eagle Court.

It is a curious coincidence that the last representative of the Lemann family in London, the late Brother George Keene Lemann, joined the Caveac Lodge, and became Master in 1873. His brother, Mr. Lemann, of Plymouth, has courteously furnished me with his photograph through Bro. Matveieff, P.M., a friend of the family.

The present Vestry Clerk of the Parish of St. Bennet Finck, Mr. F. H. Pullen, very kindly afforded me much valuable information as to the Parish Records, &c., and he also introduced me to a Mr. Wm. White, Auctioneer, of 21, Great Winchester Street, who is upwards of 90 years old and had passed his early days in the Parish. The gentleman turned out to be a Freemason, a member of the "Royal Somerset House and Inverness Lodge, No. 4," and I must say that not the least distinction that ancient lodge can claim is having had as a member a Brother so venerable and courteous. Brother White was engaged, apparently, in some complicated accounts when I was shewn into his room. These he kindly laid aside, and I put before him Stow's Survey for 1750, the engravings of St. Bennet Finck and other papers. I then followed, really with amazement, the clear and concise account of places, inhabitants, and events of some 80 years ago. The small print on the plan had no difficulties for Brother White who could read it more easily than I could. "Yes, I think," said Brother White, "this plan shows very

"well how the streets stood in 1821. That was when my
"father took the 'Edinburgh Castle' Inn in Sweeting's Rents,
"just west of the church and facing the Exchange. On the
"east side of the church was Spread Eagle Court. In my
"time there was no Tavern in the Court itself, but the 'Fleece
"and Sun' was at the corner."

"This Tavern was next to the premises then occupied
"by Mr. Lemann, a Frenchman, as a biscuit shop and
"manufactory. I believe this old business is still carried on
"at 28, St. Swithin's Lane. There, at the south end of
"Sweeting's Rents, nearer Cornhill, was a little newspaper
"shop. Francis Moon was an errand boy there and used
"to sweep out the shop in the morning. He prospered and
"set up for himself as a stationer in that shop, at the corner
"of Threadneedle Street and Finch Lane. He was an
"excellent man of business, and when there was a rumour
"of the rebuilding of the Royal Exchange and the streets
"adjacent, he invested in freeholds, and 99 year's leases, and
"so his executors now own most of the property to the east
"of the Exchange. He was afterward Lord Mayor.
"Certainly I remember the family of Howard in the parish.
"They were well known, and one had a fishmonger's shop
"in Threadneedle Street; we used to get all our fish there.
"I am not the Wm. White, Innkeeper, who was initiated
"into your Caveac Lodge in 1787, that is a little before my
"time. He may have been a relation, but my father's name
"was James."

Some portion of this conversation no doubt does not immediately relate to the subject matter of this history, but I think I need not apologise for setting out the gist of it at length. Brother Wm. White may not be the oldest Mason in England, but with regard to memory and capacity as a nonagenarian I feel assured he must take the first place.

## CHAPTER IV.

### THE HISTORY OF THE CAVEAC LODGE SINCE 1768.

AS Hammersmith was the home of the Lodge from 1768 to 1849, a few words as to this old Suburb will not be here out of place.

The best authorities I can find dealing with the locality are Bowack's *Antiquities of Middlesex* (1705), Faulkner's *History of Hammersmith* (1839), and the Cassell's *Old and New London and Suburbs*.

The ancient name of Hammersmith in the Doomsday Book is Hermoderwode. The earliest record of the name "Hamersmith" spelt with one "m" appears in the Court Rolls of the time of Henry VII., and this spelling continued in these Rolls down to 1820. It was originally part of the Parish of Fulham, but the Parishes were divided in 1834.

Bowack in his *Antiquities of Middlesex*, referring to Hammersmith in 1705, describes it as a village situated on the Thames, and extending north as far as the Great Western Road. Having many good houses in and about it inhabited by the gentry and persons of quality, and in the summer forming a retreat for the nobility and wealthy citizens of London.

Indeed, we can well imagine it at that time as a very pleasant place indeed, with its quaint houses, and beautiful old Church looking towards the river. It was prosperous, too,

VIEW OF HAMMERSMITH (1770).

famous for its Market Gardens, Orchards, and other industries. Bradley in his *Philosophical Account of the Works of Nature* (1721) says, " The Gardens about Hammersmith are famous for strawberries and such like fruit, and Mr. Millett's Garden at the North End affords cherries, apricots, and curiosities of all kinds some months before the natural season."

The town was not cut off from the outer world, or the great City to the East, as two Highways met there, and the arrival and departure of coaches, and passenger waggons kept its many old inns gay and busy. Even in winter it had its charm, as we find Thomson was then a frequent visitor at the old " Dove Coffee House " on the Bank side, and wrote most of his " *Winter* " there. It may be presumed that the following verses were composed when contemplating the river from the bow window of his room :—

" The loosened ice
Let down the flood, and half dispersed by day.
Rustles no more, but to the sedgy bank
Fast grows or gathers round the pointed shore.
A crystal pavement by the breath of Heaven
Cemented firm, till seized from shore to shore
The whole imprisoned river grows below "

In Murray's Environs of London (page 30) we find " in the early part of the 19th century there was a pleasant cottage called ' The Seasons,' an appendage of ' The Doves,' and the favourite smoking resort of the M.W. Grand Master the Duke of Sussex, who is said to have kept there a choice assortment of meerschaums." According to Lyson's History of Middlesex " The Seasons " was later known as " Sussex House."

The village of 1705 grew to be a town during the 18th century, and the tombstones and tablets in the church show that numerous citizens of London had removed there during this period. In 1801 there were 871 houses in the Parish, and in 1831 as many as 1712, but doubtless this increase was due in a great measure to the opening of the Suspension Bridge.

Residences began to be built early in the 18th Century at frequent intervals all along the High Road leading from Kensington to Hammersmith. And close to Lee's Nursery Samuel Taylor Coleridge stopped with his friends the Morgans. Crabb Robinson, in his diary dated 28th July, 1811, says, "after dining walked to Morgans beyond Kensington to see Coleridge and found Southey there."

The Inns at which the Lodge met whilst it remained at Hammersmith were the " Windsor Castle," the " Bell and Anchor," " The Angel," the " Coffee House," Broadway, and the " Royal Sussex " Hotel.

The " Windsor Castle " where the Lodge first met in 1768 is an old Coaching Inn on the north side of the King's Road, about 300 yards from the Broadway. As far as I can ascertain the old House has scarcely undergone any alteration. The room in which the Lodge probably met is seen in the photograph to the left, and abutting on to the road. It is still used for Masonic meetings.

The " Bell and Anchor " was also a famous Coaching Inn on the North Road. In Faulkner's History this Inn is thus described as it appeared in 1839, when our Lodge was meeting there. "Adjoining the Turnpike on the west is situate the " Bell and Anchor " Tavern. The house has long been used by the magistrates for holding the Petty Sessions of the Kensington Division of the 100 of Ossulston for which purpose it is particularly well adapted, being centrally situated as regards the Parishes of Acton, Brentford, Hammersmith, Fulham, Chelsea, and Kensington, and their Worships the Magistrates have ever found it convenient for business,

VIEW OF WINDSOR CASTLE INN, HAMMERSMITH

the rooms being appropriately fitted up and arranged. The various rooms in the house are ornamented with Chinese and other Oriental drawings collected by the proprietor during his voyages in the East Indies. During the early part of the reign of George III. this house was much frequented by the nobility and gentry and several humorous caricatures respecting this place, and its visitors were published by Bowles and Carver, Saint Paul's Churchyard." There is also an engraving of the old house on page 238 of Faulkner's History.

The "Angel" is also a very old Inn of somewhat smaller accommodation, situated in King Street, about 200 yards from the "Windsor Castle" Hotel, but has lost most of its original features.

The King's Coffee House has disappeared. This was "the Coffee House" where the Grand Master the Duke of Sussex dined with the Lodge in 1825, after laying the foundation stone of the bridge. I shall have to refer again to this incident in the history of the Lodge a little later on.

The "Royal Sussex" Hotel is still extant at the corner of the Broadway, but is entirely modernised.

Parish records are, as a rule, curiously perverse and annoying, in that they generally commence a few years after the period you wish to investigate. So, in Hammersmith, the rate books, &c., prior to 1793 have been lost. Mr. S. Martin, the chief librarian of the Hammersmith Public Library, has kindly ascertained for me that, in 1793, Anthony Newman (made a member of the Lodge 1785) was then owner and proprietor of the "Windsor Castle" Hotel. A Mr. Rhodes (succeeding a Mr. Rusworth) was owner of the "Bell and Anchor," and William White (made a member of the Lodge in 1787) was the owner of "The Angel," later on Bro. Starbuck became the proprietor.

Referring back for a moment here to the disappearance of Mrs. Ann Bowles of the "Caveac Tavern" from the City in 1768, I find in the Burial Registers of Hammersmith Parish these two entries :

"John Bowles buried 13th December, 1770."

"Ann Bowles buried 21st April, 1785, aged 64."

But I cannot find where this Ann Bowles resided in the Parish, nor identify her with any of the Hammersmith Inns.

The official lists of members of the Lodge, from the records of Grand Lodge, have been obtained from 1768 to 1848, and when completed from the Minute books to date, will be bound and kept by the Secretary.

And now with regard to the brethren meeting at these old Hammersmith Inns. As I mentioned before, the first Master and Senior and Junior Wardens of the Lodge in the warrant were respectively John Maddocks, Henry Adams, and Vaughan. They do not appear in the first returns to Grand Lodge, and I cannot trace their connection with Hammersmith. They may have all three been members of the old Caveac Lodge meeting at the Tavern, or possibly they were experienced Masons who undertook to put the brethren on the true Masonic line and rule, and then retired. No doubt there existed at that time a class of what may be termed "professional Masons"—I do not use the word in any disparaging sense — of whom, perhaps, the distinguished Bro. Thomas Dunckerley, was an excellent type.

I have, however, endeavoured to trace the identity of these three Brethren by reference to the Obituaries for the period published by the Harleian Society, and two curious little books entitled Kent's "Complete Guide, 1740," and Baldwin's "Complete Guide to the City of London and its

Inhabitants, 1770." I have found, however, from other researches that these latter works sadly belie their title, and are in fact very incomplete. The only names I can find which would correspond as to date, &c., to these Brethren I give below, mentioning them only as a matter of record, and with a view to possible future verification :—

JOHN MADDOCKS
> Died 24th September, 1794, at his seat at Mount Maxall, near Bexley, Kent, at an advanced age. At the time of his death he was a King's Counsel, and a Bencher of Lincoln's Inn and the Middle Temple. He married in May, 1758, a daughter of J. Whitechurch, Esq., of Twickenham. (Gent. Mag. 760.)
>
> There was also living in 1770 a John Maddocks, of 10, Bearbinder Lane, near the Mansion House, Stockbroker. (Baldwin's Guide.)
>
> Henry Adams, of 78, Mark Lane, a well-known City Attorney, died there, 1st July, 1793. (Gent. Mag. 837.)
>
> Henry Vaughan, died at his residence, Twickenham, 8th September, 1775. (Gent. Mag. 455.)

There were nine Founders of the Lodge, namely :— Thomas Hallet, Thomas Algar, John Drippe, Stephen Randall, John Wilson, Daniel Oxeland, Thomas Yean, William Harvey, and Richard Loveday.

Looking through the first list of members one cannot but be struck with the apparently humble occupations that some of them followed. We notice in the description " Bricklayer," " Carpenter," " Mason," &c., often occurring. But in our day they would have been styled " Brick Manufacturer and Contractor," " Builder " and " Architect." These were

Freeholders, and gentlemen of repute to whom we owe the erection of many of the beautiful old mansions in the neighbourhood, and along the river bank. And here one cannot but be reminded of one of the most interesting problems of earlier Masonic History. The question as to who were the actual designers, and architects of our cathedrals, monasteries, and old historic mansions? For the answer Brethren could not do better than read Chapter VI. on " Medieval Operative Masonry," in W. Bro. Gould's History ; where, after much interesting matter, he arrives at the conclusion that the architects were superior mechanics, or master masons ; sometimes aided by what may be termed amateur ecclesiastical architects.

Of the nine Founders of the Lodge, some of their names appear in the Parish records as churchwardens, trustees of charities, etc., yet only one perhaps has left behind him any notable record. The one exception is *Richard Loveday*, Surgeon. The many virtues of our Brother are recorded in a large marble tablet in the Parish Church. I cannot refrain from setting the inscription out at length, as I think possibly he was the first Secretary of the Lodge at Hammersmith.

M. S.
Ricardi Loveday Armigeri
Qui hac in villa per annos fere quadraginta
In arte medica felicissime et humanissime sese exercuit.
Vir fuit si quis alius
Mores cujus faciles innocentes simplices
Ingenium liberale sinarum pium.
Omnes sibi divincerunt
In humile spe beatæ resurrectionis
Obiit Xmo dici Decembris Anno Christi
MDCCXII. Ætatis suæ LXXXI.

Brother Loveday it would seem therefore had only just settled in Hammersmith when he became a Founder. Possibly he had removed from the City. I note that there was at that time a Stationer residing at Fish Street Hill, City, close to Finch Lane, named John Loveday, who died 7th September, 1786. Possibly this was his father.

In going through the names of the first members, apart from the founders, it is seldom after this long lapse of time that I can revive any facts at once certain, and interesting in their lives. We get, however, a glimpse now and then in the Parish records, and histories which may be entertaining to their successors in the Lodge, and for the sake of clearness I will head each paragraph with the name of the brother.

JOHN GOMME, aged 26, Carpenter, Hammersmith, 6 5/1773.

In our day he would have called himself a builder. He was the owner of land to the north of the High Road opposite the convent. and a trustee of two of the Parish charities.

In Cassell's History, Vol. VI., page 532, it is recorded that "In June, 1780, during the Gordon 'no Popery' Riots, the mob attacked the Nunnery or Convent of 'The little Sisters of the Poor.' The only precaution the sisters seem to have taken was to pack up the sacramental plate in a chest which the Lady Abbess entrusted to a faithful friend and neighbour, a Mr. Gomme, who kindly buried it in his garden till the danger had passed away."

Our brother doubtless incurred some risk for becoming the safe repository of the plate. So all honour to his memory for assisting the weak against the strong. The convent still remains in a modern building to the south of the high road, near St. Paul's School.

The mention of mobs reminds me that Hammersmith was not always the pleasant and peaceable suburb that one delights in fancying it. Queen Caroline occupied Brandenburg House, Hammersmith, for some time previous to, and during her Trial, and died there 11th August, 1821. Her funeral took place on the 14th August, and the inhabitants, who greatly sympathised with her misfortunes, desired to follow the funeral procession. The military, however, had orders to prevent this, and a free fight took place all along the road, terminating in a regular battle opposite Kensington Church and in Hyde Park, the mob here trying to compel the procession to pass through the City. Swords and pistols were used, and several on both sides killed and wounded. A tablet in Hammersmith Church was erected to two of the inhabitants, named Honey and Francis, who fell in this disturbance.

JOHN SICH, aged 26, Brewer, Chiswick, 1 3 1774.

A member of the still famous firm of Messrs. Sich & Co., of the Lamb Brewery, Chiswick. They are the owners of the "Windsor Castle" Inn. Bro. Sich was born at South Ockenden, Essex, in 1751, and became partner in the brewery in 1773, and in 1778 married Miss Ann Ruberry.

In Chiswick parish church we find this tablet.
Beneath, in a vault,
are deposited the remains of
JOHN SICH, Esq.,
for more than 60 years
an inhabitant of this parish.
He died 24th January, 1836, aged 86 years.

JOHN SICH.
(INITIATED 1774: DIED 1836—62 YEARS A MEMBER OF THE LODGE.)

I gather from the lists and Treasurer's Accounts, that this Brother remained a member of the lodge until his death, a period of 62 years. No doubt he was Master of the lodge.

The portrait of Bro. Sich is taken from a silhouette kindly supplied by his grandson, Mr. Alexander Sich, of Chiswick.

EDWARD SPEER aged 36, Whitesmith, Hammersmith, 5/4/1774.

We read in Faulkner's History, page 261. " In this Row (Brook Lane) resided Mr. Edward Speer, ironmonger and smith, who was born on the 4th June, 1738, the birthday of His late Majesty George III. and nearly at the same hour. He was also married on the same day and died nearly the same hour as the King, namely, on Saturday evening, January 29th, 1820 at about 9 o'clock, aged 82. This family has been resident inhabitants of the town since the reign of Queen Elizabeth."

JOHN BROWN, aged 28, Butcher, Hammersmith, 4/4/1775.

There is a tablet to the memory of this Brother in Hammersmith Church.

SACRED to the MEMORY of JOHN BROWN,
late of
Brandenburg Cottage,
Who departed this life November, 8th 1823.

By his will dated the 17th July, 1822, he establishes a Charitable Trust still existing. He gave "£2000 to be held in Trust for the poor of the Parish, and the moiety of the rent of a house in King Street, near the ' Windsor

Castle,' then in the occupation of Mr. Holmer, for the purchase of blankets for the said poor on New Year's Day."

ANTHONY TEN-BROEKE, aged 50, Gentleman, Hammersmith, joined 1782.

This Brother was a notable Freemason and his name was, even then, well known in the Masonic world as a Past Master of the Caledonian Lodge, No. 325. He was presented by this Lodge with a special Past Master's jewel "for his distinguished services," and this jewel can now be seen in the Grand Lodge Museum. Several years before his joining the Caveac Lodge a movement was started to Incorporate the Masonic Society by Royal Charter. Bro. A. Ten-Broeke headed the opposition and the scheme was abandoned.

JOHN HOWARD, aged 30, Innkeeper, Hammersmith, + 12 1787.

\* This is an interesting name. Referring back to page 27 you will see that a "John Howard" was a witness to the will of Bertrand Cahuac or Caveac, and further, that at this time and for many years before, the Howards had lived next door to the Caveac Tavern in Spread Eagle Court. Was this Brother a son of the John Howard, the old friend of Cahuac? I cannot find any mention of a family of Howard connected with Hammersmith, but in the adjoining Parish of Brentford there is a Tablet in the Parish Church "Sacred to the Memory of John Soame Howard, late of this Parish, who died 27th January, 1810, aged 52 years." I think this must be the same man, though there is a discrepancy of one year in the dates.

THOMAS JULLION, aged 23, Attorney, Brentford, 23 4 1789.

In Brentford Parish Church there is a tablet to the memory of this brother, the first lawyer to join the Lodge.

"Mr. Thomas Jullion, thirty-eight years vestry clerk of this parish, died July 13th, 1838, aged 70 years."

ROBERT WEST, 32, Baker, Hammersmith, 1801.

This Brother was a trustee of several of the parish charities, and afterwards served the office of churchwarden.

GEORGE BIRD, 30, Bricklayer, Hammersmith, 1804.

This Brother was a considerable freeholder and trustee of parish charities. He owned a large brick field between Hammersmith and Shepherd's Bush, and was afterwards one of the contractors for the Suspension Bridge.

Bro. Bird was Treasurer of the Lodge in 1823.

So much for the earlier lists of members.

The years from 1804 to 1815 or thereabouts, saw a marked increase in the Members of the Lodge, but apparently no one of any great note. We find that they held the offices of churchwardens, parish clerks, trustees, &c., but it would be wearisome to record these seriatim.

In many respects the year 1823 is one of considerable importance in the Lodge records, for, from that date we may say that the authentic domestic history (for want of a better phrase) begins. The Treasurer's accounts are complete from that date, though the old Minutes prior to 1843 have, alas! departed. That these Minutes were kept is plain, as there are charges in the Treasurer's accounts prior to 1843 for new Minute books. This year is also noticeable for the fact that there were eight joining members, and nine initiates, most of them professional men. One or two were well known in the neighbourhood and did much good Masonic work.

LAWRENCE THOMPSON, Printer, Great St. Helen's, Master 1823.

This Brother had a most distinguished Masonic career. He was a Past Master of the Lodge of Antiquity and of the Royal Inverness Lodge. He was also a well known Preceptor in the Craft, and on several occasions was chosen to deliver the Prestonian Lecture. He was made Grand Deacon in 1847, and died in 1855. (Gould's History, vol. iii., p. 13).

W. Bro. Lawrence Thompson's Officers were as follows :—

>H. W. Mackreth, S.W.
>John Bowling, J.W.
>George Bird, Treasurer.
>John Millward, Secretary.
>Bro. Bowles, Tyler.

It is curious to see the name of Bowles again appearing in the Lodge History. Was this Tyler a son of the Ann Bowles, the hostess of the Caveac Tavern?

JOHN BOWLING, Surgeon, Hammersmith (joined from 75), 11th July, 1823.

This Brother was a notable person in the town, being in 1822 Churchwarden with Brother George Bird, and his name appears constantly in Faulkner's History. He is associated with one of the most interesting events in the History of the Lodge, namely, the laying of the

DUKE OF SUSSEX, GRAND MASTER 1813 to 1843.

Foundation Stone of Hammersmith Suspension Bridge, by the Grand Master the Duke of Sussex, on the 7th of May, 1825. Here is a card of admission signed by Brother Bowling as Steward.

## HAMMERSMITH BRIDGE.
The Festival
In Commemoration of
Laying the Foundation Stone
of
Hammersmith Bridge
Will take place at the Coffee House, Broadway.

Admit

Dinner on table at 5 o'clock,

J. BOWLING, Steward.

In Faukner's History, page 55, the following account of this event is given. "On the 7th of May, 1825, the Foundation Stone of the North Tower was laid by his Royal Highness the Duke of Sussex, with Masonic ceremony. The coffer dam being filled up as an amphitheatre in which the stone was suspended. At 4 o'clock the Royal Duke arrived, the Officers of the Grand Lodge assembled at the Latymer School Room and the Lodge was opened by the Master and Officers of the Caveac Lodge No. 231 (sic). The procession then walked from the school room to the Broadway down Angel Lane in Masonic order. On arriving at the entrance the procession divided and took their station right and left and the Duke passed to the platform. The ceremony of laying the stone commenced after three cheers had been given for his Royal Highness. The Grand Treasurer delivered to him a bottle containing the coins of the reigning sovereign, also a brass plate to be placed over the cavity with the following inscription: "The foundation stone of the bridge of suspension over the River Thames from the Hamlet of Hammersmith, in the County of Middlesex, to Barnes in Surrey, was laid with due Masonic ceremony by his Royal Highness the Duke of Sussex, Most Worshipful Grand Master, on Saturday May 7th, 1825. W. T. Clark, engineer, George Wm. and Stephen Bird and Captain Brown, Royal Marines, contractors. Mr. Robert Holt P. G. Secretary, Clerk and Secretary." On the stone being lowered the Duke scattered the corn and said "As I have poured the corn, oil and wine, emblems of wealth, plenty and comfort, so may the bridge tend to communicate prosperity and wealth from one end of the island to the other. God bless the King." The procession then returned in the same order, and his Royal Highness dined with a numerous company at the Coffee House. And so, perhaps, as Mr. Pepys would say to "The Seasons" where the Meerschaums were kept for a quiet smoke.

The old Tyler's Sword borne before the Grand Master on this occasion, is still used by the Tyler of the lodge on Installation nights, and special occasions. It has upon it the two inscriptions: "The gift of Brother Thomas Jones to the Caveac Lodge, 1787," and "Bro. Lawrence Thompson, installed Master, August 19th, 1823; Henry William Mackreth, S.W.; and John Bowling, J.W." Bro. Thomas Jones was initiated in the lodge 1780.

There is a curious entry in the Treasurer's book for 1827—

"Younds Balance of Dinner (at Coffee House)
Laying the Foundation Stone of the Bride (sic)
£39 17s. 8d."

OLD TYLER'S SWORD.

I am afraid the worthy Treasurer, George Bird, was a better contractor than speller ; but it is fair to say his accounts are clear and well made out.

It will be noticed that two of the contractors, George and Stephen Bird, were both Members of the Lodge.

Brother Bowling has the distinction of being the first Master who recorded his name as such in the books of Grand Lodge in 1827.

THOMAS CHAMBERLAIN, gentleman, Hammersmith, joined 1824.

This was probably the Brother Thomas Chamberlain, one of the original members of the Emulation Lodge of Improvement, 2nd October, 1823, and also of the Constitutional Lodge, No. 55.

JOHN DOWLEY, W. Master 1834 and 1835.

This Brother was a very distinguished Mason, a Past Master of the Burlington Lodge, No. 96. He was also one of the first members of the Emulation Lodge of Improvement, and acted as its first Treasurer from 1830 to 1833. After the death of W. Bro. Peter William Gilkes, in 1835, he became jointly with Bros. Cooper and S. Barton Wilson, Preceptor of the Lodge (See Bro. Sadler's History of the Emulation Lodge of Improvement, pages 5 and 17).

JAMES PIKE, Senior Warden, 1834.

This Brother was also a distinguished member of the Emulation Lodge of Improvement, which he joined in 1833, and is frequently mentioned in Bro. Sadler's History, and his portrait appears there, page 66.

In 1862 we find that he and W. Bros. S. B. Wilson and Thomas Fenn were appointed on the Committee. He died on the 14th May, 1870, and at the meeting of the Emulation Lodge of Improvement, on the 20th May, the ceremonies were deferred as a mark of respect to his memory. He was remarkable for his regular attendance, as from 1857 to his death he attended on no less than 582 occasions.

EDWARD GALLEY GILES (joined from No. 5), W. Master, 1838, 1843, 1844, 1846 and 1851.

There is no name that ought to be more honoured in the Caveac Lodge than that of Brother Giles. I rather gather that up to about 1840 the lodge had flourished and increased its numbers. There came a period of great depression lasting some 15 years; but Brother Giles fought hard to preserve the Lodge from collapse. He attended regularly and was Master, Treasurer, or Secretary as occasion required. The Minutes began by him in 1845 are very carefully kept, and really resemble a series of illuminated addresses as our Brother, painted and gilded the capital letters. Brother Henry Muggeridge, Preceptor of the Lodge of Stability, appears to have been his guest at the lodge on several occasions, and Brother Giles probably followed the working of that Brother.

On the 9th June, 1852, he presented the lodge with a Masonic Goblet still preserved. The last mention of Brother Giles is in the Minutes of the meeting of the 8th June, 1853, when it is stated that he had been called abroad.

ELIJAH LITCHFIELD, W. Master, 1847. Secretary, 1851 to 1875.

This Brother most zealously and ably assisted Brother Giles when everything combined to discourage and dishearten those connected with the Lodge. Happily this Brother lived to see it prosperous and flourishing again, for he only resigned the Secretaryship of the Lodge in 1875, to the universal regret of

ELIJAH LITCHFIELD, P.M.

all its members. His portrait is taken from a minature kindly lent by his daughter, Mrs. Barnes, of Harwich.

And now we come to what may be termed the modern history of the Lodge, for we see, from time to time, in the

Minutes, the names of candidates proposed who still remain, and we hope for many years will remain, esteemed members of the Lodge.

The Lodge had removed from the "Bell and Anchor," Hammersmith, in 1849, to Anderson's Hotel, Kensington,

CHARLES DOREY, P.M.

and thence, in 1856, to the "Star and Garter," Kew Bridge, and in 1862 to the "Crown and Sceptre," Greenwich. Its numbers and prospects did not materially increase. It was, however, a happy day for the Lodge, when, on the

10th June, 1857, a Mr. John William Rouse, of the Grove, Camberwell, was initiated. It was this brother who proposed on the 26th October, 1859, Mr. Charles Browne, Surgeon, of Camberwell, and Mr. Charles Dorey, Gentleman, of the same place, as initiates. These two brethren in their turn, on the 20th November, 1862, proposed Mr. Percival Alleyne Nairne, also of Camberwell.

Thus a nucleus was formed of earnest zealous Masons who soon made their influence felt, and though doubtless for many years there were grievous difficulties to encounter, yet from the period of their joining I do not think the Lodge ever really looked back in a steady advance towards the position it has now for many years held in Masonry.

On the 7th August, 1867, a warrant was granted for the formation of a Caveac Royal Arch Chapter, and on the 25th of October, in the same year, the chapter was duly consecrated, and has ever since flourished, and done good work in the Royal Arch Degree.

In writing a History such as this it is scarcely permissible to introduce one's own personal opinions, but perhaps I may be allowed here to touch upon a little matter connected with the Ritual. In the Chapter there is a small piece of Ritual which is given at the Banquet prior to the Toasts which has always seemed to me very effective, and as adding greatly to the dignity, and decorum of these gatherings. I have often thought that some Ritual of a like nature might be usefully introduced into the Craft Banquets. For instance, the Master might ask the Senior Warden to "name the Grand Principles on which the Order is founded," and afterwards request him to define these in accordance with the 6th Section of the 1st Lecture. These Definitions are short, much to the point, and form an appropriate introduction to the first Toast.

In 1868, W. Bro. P. A. Nairne, P.G.D., was Master, and on the 10th of October, 1868, a petition was drawn up and presented to Grand Lodge praying that a Centenary Warrant should be granted to the Lodge. The issue of the Warrant having been authorised by the Grand Master, it was on behalf of Grand Lodge duly presented by W. Bro. Grissell, S.G.D., at a Lodge meeting held the 13th March, 1869, numerous Grand Officers and brethren attending (copy of warrant, see Appendix I.)

After a short period of meeting at Radley's Hotel, Blackfriars, and the Westminster Palace Hotel, the Lodge moved, in 1874, to the Albion Tavern, Aldersgate Street, thus at length returning to the City where it first originated. I trust that the Lodge may now ever remain at the Albion, a most comfortable and suitable Masonic place of meeting.

At the meeting of the Lodge held on the 10th January, 1885, Bro. C. Dorey, P.M., proposed, and Bro. C. Browne, P.M., seconded a resolution " That the V.W. Reverend Robert James Simpson, M.A., P.G.C., be requested to accept an honorary membership of the Caveac Lodge in recognition of the distinguished position he occupies in Freemasonry, and of the esteem in which he is held by the brethren of the Lodge, and that he be elected an honorary member forthwith." This resolution having been put and carried unanimously, the Rev. Bro. Simpson acknowledged and accepted the same, and he was declared elected accordingly *honoris causa*. On the 12th June, 1885, he was appointed Chaplain by W. Bro. Oscar Moore, W.M. This office he held until his death in January, 1900, when he was succeeded by V.W. Bro. Archdeacon Sinclair, P.G.C.

V.W. Bro. Simpson presented to the Lodge at Christmas,

LOVING CUP.
PRESENTED BY THE REVD. R. J. SIMPSON, P.G.C., IN 1887.

1887, an antique Masonic Loving Cup supposed to be about 200 years old, and a Photograph Book for the portraits of Past Masters. The case holding the Loving Cup is now guarded by two daggers, the very kind gift to the Lodge by W. Bro. H. W. Seager of the Royal Hampton Court Lodge, who has also presented a handsome silver inkstand to the Lodge.

W. Bro. Charles Browne, P.M., was on the 13th June, 1868, appointed Director of Ceremonies, and on the 12th May, 1877, W. Bro. P A. Nairne was appointed Treasurer. At the meeting of the Lodge on the 14th December, 1901, W. Bro. D. T. Tudor, Worshipful Master, a presentation was made and an address presented to these two worthy brethren as some slight recognition of their most valuable services to the Lodge for so many years.

W. Bro. Nairne, to the great regret of the Lodge, resigned his office of Treasurer in December, 1903, and at the meeting of the Lodge held on the 9th January, 1904, the following resolution was proposed by W. Bro. R. Davies, I.P.M., and seconded by W. Bro. Charles Browne, P.M., D.C., and unanimously carried. " That the best thanks of this Lodge be presented to W. Bro. P. A. Nairne, P.G.D., P.M., for his eminent services to the Lodge in the capacity of Treasurer for twenty-two years, services which in the opinion of the brethren have been of the very highest value, and have largely conduced to the success of the Lodge." This address signed by all the officers of the Lodge was afterwards suitably engraved, and presented to Bro. Nairne.

The successor to Bro. Nairne in the office of Treasurer was W. Bro. Mihill Slaughter, P.A.G.D.C., P.M., a Brother to whom the Lodge is much indebted for advice on all Masonic matters, including the Ritual.

After Bro. Litchfield resigned, in 1875, the office of

Secretary, it devolved on W. Bro. Charles Dorey, P.M., who zealously performed the duties till his lamented death in 1889. To him succeeded W. Bro. W. M. Goss, P.M., who, to the regret of the Lodge, had to relinquish his office from ill-health in 1900, and was then made an Honorary Member. The office was then held by Bro. Slaughter till 1904, and is now held by W. Bro. J. White, P.M.

The above paragraphs relating to the recent History of the Lodge were written by me early in the present month of February, and I think it better that they should stand unaltered. Since, however, they were completed, the Lodge has sustained a grievous loss in the death of our esteemed Brother Dr. Charles Browne, P.M. and D.C., the Father of the Lodge, who passed suddenly away on the 21st of February.

Brother Browne was a Member of the Lodge for nearly half a century. He had a striking and unique personality. In the Lodge his genial reception of Visitors, his kindly and tactful speeches on all occasions, and his rendering of the Address to the Members on Installation nights were alike admirable, and perfect patterns for imitation. And outside the Lodge none so ready as he to drop the tear of sympathy over the failings of a Brother, and to pour the healing balm of consolation into the wounds of the afflicted.

Many of the Past Masters and Brethren attended at the Brookwood Cemetery on Saturday, the 25th of February, to pay the last sad tribute to one of whom it can be truly said that he lived respected, and died regretted by all who knew him.

Bro. Browne's portrait forms the Frontispiece to this volume, and represents him in his robes as "Master of the Society of Apothecaries."

I think it may serve a useful purpose to give a short

summary of the position of the Lodge with regard to the three Masonic Charities :—

*Royal Masonic Institution for Boys.*
Subscribed by Lodge £133 7s. from 1861 to 1901.
The Lodge is Vice-President of the Institution, and entitled to 17 votes.

*Royal Masonic Institution for Girls.*
Subscribed by Lodge £99 5s. from 1863 to 1904.
The Lodge is £5 5s. short of the contribution qualifying it as Vice-President, and is now entitled to 12 votes.

*Royal Masonic Benevolent Institution.*
Subscribed by Lodge to Widows' Fund, £42.
Subscribed by Lodge to Mens' Fund, £41 10s.
Entitled to 12 votes for Widows, and 10 for Men.

In the appendix will be found a list of Past Masters, but for the reasons mentioned in the note at the head of the list, the names of the earlier ones are mostly wanting. We have now living twenty-two Past Masters of the Lodge, seven of whom are country members. For many years the average attendance of the Past Masters has been very satisfactory, as many as sixteen turning up on Installation nights. I think this excellent, and desirable result has been attained by the general observance of some simple, and unwritten rules relative to the work. Roughly speaking they are as follows :—

(1.) The Master is expected, if occasion offers, to perform once, at any rate during his year of office, all the Craft ceremonies, including explanation of Tracing Board, and the general ceremony of installing his successor.

(2.) When at a meeting there are two or more ceremonies, one of which he has already performed, he is expected to delegate that to a Past Master.

(3.) If a Past Master proposes a Candidate for Initiation he should have the option of performing the ceremony.

(4.) When there is no ceremony the Master is expected to call upon two or three Past Masters to assist him in working Sections of a Lecture.

(5.) At the Installation the addresses to the Master, Wardens, and brethren, are given by Past Masters or some distinguished visitor to the Lodge. On the last occasion, the V.W. the Grand Secretary being present, most kindly gave the address to the Master.

Thus, by keeping up the interest of the Past Masters in the Lodge and the ritual of Masonry, harmony is promoted and prosperity assured.

The number of Members of the Lodge on the list stands at present at 59, of whom some 16 are Honorary or Country Members. It has been thought well to—if possible—restrict the number of Full members to 45. Those having the welfare of the Lodge at heart have felt that numbers, and wealth are not the true tests of the prosperity, and progress of any Lodge. And though one would be reluctant indeed to exclude any—if worthy—from the benefits of Freemasonry, yet the utmost care should be taken to admit those, and only those who will be likely to appreciate fully the ancient Landmarks of the Order, and uphold the Great Principles which it inculcates.

PAST MASTERS AND CENTENARY JEWELS.

## APPENDIX I.

Beaufort G.M. (*Original Warrant.*)

No. 424.

TO all and every, our Right Worshipful Worshipful and Loving Brethren, WE, His Grace Henry Somerset, Duke of Beaufort, Marquis and Earl of Worcester, Earl of Glamorgan, Visct. Grosmont, Baron Herbert, Lord of Ragland, Chepston and Gower, all in Monmouthshire ; also Baron Beaufort, of Caldecot Castle, *Grand Master* of the Most Ancient and Honourable Society of Free and Accepted Masons send Greeting.

KNOW ye that we on the Humble Petition of our Right Worshipful and well-beloved Brethren John Maddocks, Henry Adams,    Vaughan, and several other Brethren residing at or near the Town of Hammersmith, in the County of Middlesex, Do hereby institute the said Brethren into a regular Lodge of Free and Accepted Masons to be Opened at the sign of the Windsor Castle, in the Town of Hammersmith aforesaid. And do further at their said Petition and of the great Trust and Confidence reposed in every of the said above Named Three Brethren Do hereby appoint John Maddocks to be Master, Henry Adams, Senior Warden, and    Vaughan, Junior Warden, for Opening the said Lodge, and for such further time only as shall be thought proper by the Brethren thereof, it being Our Will that this Our appointment of the above Officers shall in no wise Affect any future Election of Officers of the Lodge ; but that such Election shall be regulated agreeable to such Bye-Laws of the said Lodge as shall be consistant with the General Laws of this Society contained in the Book of Constitutions. AND we hereby Will and Require you, the said John Maddocks, to take Special Care that all and every the said Bretbren are or have been regularly made Masons, and that they do Observe, Perform, and keep all the Rules and Orders contained in the Book of Constitutions.

And further that you do from time to time cause to be entered in a Book kept for that Purpose an Account in Writing of your Proceedings in the Lodge together with all such Rules, Orders and Regulations as shall be made for the good Government of the same, that in no wise you Omit once in every year to send to Us or Our Successors, Grand Masters, or to The Honourable Charles Dillon, Esquire, Our Deputy Grand Master, or to the Deputy Grand Master for the time being, an Account in Writing of your said proceedings and Copies of all such Rules, Orders and Regulations as shall be made as aforesaid, together with a list of the Members of the Lodge and such a Sum of Money as may suit the circumstances of the Lodge and reasonably be expected towards the Grand Charity. Moreover, we hereby Will and Require you the said John Maddocks as soon as conveniently may be to send an Account in Writing of what shall be done by Virtue of these Presents.

GIVEN at *London* under the Hand and Seal of *Masonry* this 21st day of May, A.D. 1768, A.L. 5768.

*By the Grand Master's Command,*

   (Signed)  CHARLES DILLON,

              D.G.M

Witness :

(Signed)  SAMUEL SPENCER,

       G.S.

N.B.—On the back is written "Caveac Lodge, Constitution Roll."

---

## ZETLAND G.M. (*Centenary Warrant*).

To the Master, Wardens, other Officers and Members of the Caveac Lodge, No. 176, London, and all others whom it may concern.

*Greeting.* *Whereas* it appears by the Records of the Grand Lodge that on the 21st May, 1768, a Warrant of Constitution was granted to certain Brethren therein named, authorizing and empowering them and their regular Successors to hold a Lodge of Free and Accepted Masons at the Windsor Castle, at Hammersmith, in the County of Middlesex, and which Lodge was there registered as No. 425. But in consequence of the Union of the two Grand Lodges, and the formation of the United Grand Lodge on the 27th December, 1813, it became No. 233, since which owing to the general alteration in the numbers, it has become and now stands on the Registry as No. 176, and meeting at Radley's Hotel, New Bridge Street, Blackfriars, in the City of London, under the Title or Denomination of

### THE CAVEAC LODGE.

AND WHEREAS the Brethren composing the said Lodge are desirous, now that it has completed the CENTENARY of its existence, to be permitted to wear a jewel commemorative of such event, and have prayed one sanction for that purpose.

NOW KNOW YE that we having taken the subject into our consideration, have acceded to their request, and in virtue of our prerogative DO HEREBY GIVE AND GRANT possession to all and each of the actual subscribing members of the said Lodge being Master Masons to wear in all Masonic Meetings suspended to the left breast by a sky-blue ribbon not exceeding one inch and a half in breadth, a JEWEL or MEDAL of the pattern or device that we have already approved of as a CENTENARY JEWEL. But such jewel is to be worn only by those Brethren who are *bonâ-fide* subscribing members of the said Lodge, and for so long only as each shall pay his regular stipulated subscription to the funds thereof and be duly returned as such to the Grand Lodge of England.

Given at London this 3rd November, A.L. 5868, A.D. 1868.

By COMMAND of the Most Worshipful Grand Master the RIGHT HONORABLE THE EARL OF ZETLAND.

(Signed)   JOHN HERVEY,

G.S.

N.B.—The number in the Warrant is 424, but in the Register of Grand Lodge it is 425.

## APPENDIX II.

*List of Meeting Places of the Caveac Lodge. No. 176.*

1755 to 1768—Caveac Tavern, Spread Eagle Court, Finch Lane.

1768 to 1772—Windsor Castle Hotel, Hammersmith.
1772 to 1786—Bell and Anchor, ,,
1786 to 1823—Angel Inn, ,,
1823 to 1833—Coffee House, Broadway, ,,
1833 to 1836—Windsor Castle Hotel, ,,
1836 to 1839—Royal Sussex Hotel ,,
1839 to 1849—Bell and Anchor ,,
1849 to 1856—Anderson's Hotel, Kensington.
1856 to 1862—Star and Garter Hotel, Kew Bridge.
1862 to 1866—Crown and Sceptre Tavern, Greenwich.
1866 to 1872—Radley's Hotel, Bridge Street, Blackfriars.
1872 to 1874—Westminster Palace Hotel, Westminster.
1874 to date—Albion Tavern, Aldersgate Street, City.

## APPENDIX III.

*List of Numbers given to the Lodge from time to time.*

Caveac Lodge was, in the year 1755, numbered 86.

Caveac Lodge was, in the year 1768, numbered 425.
,, ,, ,, 1770, 360.
,, ,, ,, 1780, 270.
,, ,, ,, 1791, 277.
,, ,, ,, 1792, 232.
,, ,, ,, 1814, 292.
,, ,, ,, 1832, 295.
,, ,, ,, 1863, 170.

# APPENDIX IV.

## Past Masters of the Lodge.

(The Lists of Members at Grand Lodge do not indicate the Masters of the Lodge, and there are no signatures of Masters or Wardens prior to 1827. The Installation was in June until 1889, when it was altered to January.)

| | | |
|---|---|---|
| 1767. | William Acton | Master (Caveac Tavern.) |
| 1768. | John Maddocks | ,, (Windsor Castle.) |
| | John Sich | ,, |
| | George Bird | ,, |
| 1823. | Lawrence Thompson, | P.G.D. |
| 1824. | H. W. Mackreth | Master. |
| 1827. | John Bowling | ,, |
| 1833. | Joseph Millward | ,, |
| 1834. | John Dowley ⎫ | |
| | James Pike ⎭ | S.W. |
| 1835. | John Dowley | Master. |
| 1836. | James Bird | ,, |
| 1837. | George Warriner | ,, |
| 1838. | Edward Galley Giles | . |
| 1839. | John Osbertus Truman | ,, |
| 1840. | William McMullen | , |
| 1841. | John A. L. Barnard | , |
| 1842. | John Francis White | . |
| 1843. | Edward Galley Giles | ,, |
| 1844. | Edward Galley Giles | , |
| 1845. | Samuel Scott | ,, |
| 1846. | Edward Galley Giles | ,, |
| 1847. | Elijah Litchfield | , |
| 1848. | John Charles McMullen | ,, |
| 1849. | Frederick T. West | ,, |
| 1850. | Frederick T. West | ,, |
| 1851. | Edward Galley Giles | ,, |
| 1852. | R. F. Williams | ,, |

1853. R. F. Williams           Master
1854. Frederick T. West
1855. Frederick T. West        ,,
1856. Benjamin Head            ,,
1857. G. P. Salmon             ,,
1858. William Wagstaff         ,,
1859. Charles Ireland          ,,
1860. J. W. Rouse              ,,
1861. C. R. Stock
1862. T. O. Stock              ,
1863. C. T. Dorey
1864. Charles Browne           ,,
1865. Pemble Browne            ,
1866. R. Galloway
1867. Henry Dorey              ,
1868. P. A. Nairne, P.G.D.
1869. William Nelson Smith     ,
1870. Thomas Quihampton        ,,
1871. R. S. Foreman            ,
1872. Henry Besley             ,
1873. George Keene Lemann
1874. P. A. Nairne, P.G.D.
1875. J. B. Sorrell
1876. W. Miller Goss           ,
1877. Walter J. Stride         ,
1878. J. B. Sorrell (Junior)   ,
1879. Walter Neumegen          ,
1880. Alfred West Thorpe       ,
1881. Edward Freeling Johnston ,,
1882. William Kirkness         ,
1883. Robert Sutherland        ,
1884. Oscar L. W. Moore        ,,
1885. Frederick Elder          ,,
1886. Arthur N. L. Burne       ,,
1887. Edward Creaton           ,,
1889. Henry D. Maclure         ,
1890. Mihill Slaughter,
       P.A.G.D.C.              ,,
1891. George C. Dent           ,,

APPENDIX 83

| | | |
|---|---|---|
| 1892. | Ernest A. de Paiva | Master. |
| 1893-4 | Norman Morice | ,, |
| 1895. | George de Horne Vaisey | ,, |
| 1896. | William Henry Fox | ,, |
| 1897. | John Percy Simpson | ,, |
| 1898. | John White | ,, |
| 1899. | John Miller Grant (Junior) | ,, |
| 1900. | Frank B. Dent | ,, |
| 1901. | Daniel Thomas Tudor | ,, |
| 1902. | Basil Matveieff | ,, |
| 1903. | Richard Davies | ,, |
| 1904. | Frank Fehr | ,, |
| 1905. | Percy Still | ,, |

## APPENDIX V.

### List of Treasurers.

| | |
|---|---|
| 1766. | Bro. William Acton. |

| | |
|---|---|
| 1823 to 1840. | Bro. George Bird (Initiated 1804.) |
| 1840 to 1843. | ,, E. G. Giles, P.M. |
| 1843. | ,, John Francis White, P.M. |
| 1844 to 1851. | ,, E. G. Giles, P.M. |
| 1851 to 1862. | ,, F. J. West, P.M. |
| 1862 to 1864. | ,, Charles Rankin Stock, P.M. |
| 1864 to 1868. | ,, Robert Galloway, P.M. |
| 1868 to 1877. | ,, Pemble Browne, P.M. |
| 1877 to 1881. | ,, Percival Alleyne Nairne, P.M. |
| 1881 to 1885. | ,, Walter J. Stride, P.M. |
| 1885 to 1904. | ,, Percival Alleyne Nairne, P.M. |
| 1904. | ,, Mihill Slaughter, P.M. |

## APPENDIX VI.

*List of Secretaries.*

| | |
|---|---|
| 1768 to | Bro. John Loveday, Surgeon. |
| 1823 to 1845. | ,, Joseph Millward (Head Master of the Latymer Schools.) |
| 1845 to 1847. | ,, John Francis White, P.M. |
| 1847 to 1852. | ,, Edward Galley Giles, P.M. |
| 1852 to 1875. | ,, Elijah Litchfield, P.M. |
| 1875 to 1889. | ,, Charles Dorey, P.M. |
| 1889 to 1900. | ,, W. Miller Goss, P.M. |
| 1900 to 1904. | ,, Mihill Slaughter, P.M. |
| 1904. | ,, John White, P.M. |

# GENERAL INDEX.

Adams, Henry (S.W. 1768)   13, 46
Acton, William (Master 1767)   ...   ...   7, 28
Albion Tavern, Aldersgate Street   ...   ...   5, 68
Algar, Thomas—Founder  ...   47
Anderson's Hotel, Kensington   66
Angel Inn, Hammersmith ...   45
"Antients"   ...   ...   6, 29
Antiquity, Lodge of, No. 2 ...   56
Baldwin, Directory of London (1770)   ...   ...   46
Bank of England Lodge   ...   14
Bannister, Butcher ...   31, 32
Barnes, Mrs. ...   ...   ...   65
Beddington, Surrey   24, 25, 27
Bell & Anchor Inn, Hammersmith   ...   ...   ...   42
Bird, George (Treasurer)   55, 62, 63
Bird, Stephen   ...   ...   63
Bluecoat Tavern   ...   ...   20
Bowack's Antiquities of Middlesex   ...   ...   ...   38
Bowles, Ann (Caveac Tavern)   29, 30, 46, 56
Bowles, John (died Hammersmith, 1770)   ...   ...   46
Bowles, Tyler to Lodge, 1823   56
Bowling, John (Master 1827) 56, 59
Bradley's Philosophical Account of the Works of Nature   ...   ...   ...   41

Brandenburg House, Hammersmith   ...   ...   50
Bridges, Revd. Canon   ...   28
Broad Street Ward ...   7, 21, 28
Brown, Dr. Charles, P.M.  67, 70, 72
Brown, John ...   ...   ...   53
Bull Inn, Leadenhall Street   13

Cahuac, Bertrand   ...   18—29
Cahuac, Bertrand (son of John)   ...   ...   26, 27
Cahuac, James   ...   25—28
Cahuac, John ...   ...   26—28
Cahuac, Martha   ...   ...   27
Cahuac, Sarah   ...   ...   27
Cahuac, Zachariah   ...   ...   30
Cahusac, Louis   ...   ...   19
Caledonian Lodge, No. 325...   54
Callow's "Old London Taverns"   ...   ...   31, 32
Castle Lodge of Harmony, No. 26   ...   ...   ...   7
Castle Lodge, Putney   ...   14
Caveac Tavern, 6, 14, 15, 19 —29, 32, 30—37, 46, 56
Centenary Warrant ...   68, 77
Chadwell's Coffee House   ...   20
Chamberlain, Thomas   ...   63

## INDEX

Chaplains of Lodge ... ... 65
Churchwardens Accounts (St. Bennet Finck) ... 16, 23
Clark, Thomas ... ... 31
Clark, Tierney W. (Engineer) 60
Coaches to Hammersmith, 18th Century ... ... 9
Coffee House, Hammersmith, 42, 45, 60
Coleridge, Samuel Taylor ... 42
Constitutional Lodge, No. 55 63
Contumvirate Society ... 7
Cooper, Alexander ... ... 31
Crabb, Robinson ... ... 42
Crow, Thomas ... ... 31
Crown & Sceptre, Greenwich 66
Crucefex, Robert ... ... 23

Davies, Richard, P.M. ... ?
Defoe, Daniel... ... 8, 9
Degremont, Rev., B.A. ... 19
Desaguliers, Rev. J. T. ... 6
Dorey, Charles, P.M. 67, 68, 72
Dove Coffee House, Hammersmith ... ... ... 41
Dowley, John, Master 1835... 63
Drew & Co. ... ... ... 36
Drippe, John, Founder ... 47
Dunckerley, Thomas ... 46

Edinburgh Castle Inn, Royal Exchange ... ... 37
Edis, John (Caveac Tavern) 31
Edis, Mary ... ... ... 31
Eloy, Peter T. ... ... 27

Emulation Lodge of Improvement ... ... 63, 64
Engraved Lists of Lodges ... 16
Evelyn, John, Diary of ... 8
Exeter Exchange, Strand ... 31

Faulkner's History of Hammersmith 38, 44, 50, 59
Finch Lane, City, 6, 7, 12, 13, 19, 28
Fisher, Cook at Caveac Tavern ... ... ... 20
Fires in City, 1666 ... 8, 9
,, ,, 1748 ... 12, 13
,, ,, 1765 ... 12, 13
Fleece and Sun, Spread Eagle Court ... 32, 35
Founders of Lodge at Hammersmith ... ... 47
Freeman's Court ... ... 8
Fulham, Parish of ... ... 38

Giles, Edward Galley, P.M.... 64
Gilkes, Peter William ... 63
Globe Lodge, No. 23 ... 14
Gomme, John ... ... 49
Gould's History of Masonry, 48, 50
Grand Lodge of England, First recorded Meeting 6
Grand Lodge of England, Minutes of, 1720 6, 7
Green, Thompson, Colonel... 1
Grissell, Henry, S.G.D., 1868 68
Guildhall Library ... ... 16

## INDEX

Hallet, Thomas (Founder) ... 47
Hammersmith, Account of 38—46
    Burial Registers ... 45
    Public Library ... 45
Harleian Society, Obituaries 46
Harvey, William (Founder) 47
Howard, John, of Spread Eagle Court ... 27, 37
Howard, John, of Hammersmith ... ... ... 54

Initiations, Performance of Ceremony ... ... 74
Irish Masons ... ... 6, 24

Jacobites ... ... ... 24
Jewels, Centenary and Past Masters ... ... ... 75
Joe's Coffee House, Finch Lane ... ... ... 32
Jones, Judith (Caveac Tavern) 30
Jones, Thomas ... ... 60
Jullion, Thomas, Attorney ... 55

Kent's Directory of London (1740) ... ... 9, 46
King's Head Tavern, Poultry 7

Latymer Schools, Hammersmith ... ... ... 50
Lectures and Sections worked 74
Le Conte, F. A ... ... 27
Lee's Nursery, Hammersmith 42
Lemann, George Keene, P.M. 35
    ,,  Michael ... ... 31
Licensing Records of London 16

Litchfield, Elijah, P.M., Secretary ... ... 64, 65
London Magazine ... ... 10
Loveday, Richard, Secretary, Hammersmith ... ... 48
Loveday, Richard, Fish Street Hill, City ... ... 49
Loving Cups presented to Lodge by E. G. Giles and Rev. R. J. Simpson 71

Mackreth, H. William, P.M., 56, 60
Maddock's, John, Master, 1768 ... ... 13, 46, 47
Masonic Charities ... ... 73
Masters of Lodge ... ... 81
Martin. S. (Hammersmith Librarian) ... ... 45
Matveieff, Basil, P.M. 1, 36
Members Present, number of 74
Merchant Taylors' Hall 6, 13
Merchant Taylors' School .. 23
Miller, Bowler (Caveac Tavern) ... ... ... 30
Millward, Joseph, Secretary 56
"Moderns" ... ... 6, 7
Moon, Sir Francis ... ... 37
Morgan, John, of Finch Lane 28
Muggeridge, Henry, Stability Lodge ... ... ... 64

Nairne. Percival Alleyne P.M., P.G.D. .. 67, 70, 71
Newman, Anthony (Windsor Castle) ... ... ... 45
Norfolk, Duke of, Grand Master, 1730 ... ... 6

## INDEX

No Popery Riots (1780) ... 40
Numbers of Lodge on Register 74
Nunnery, Hammersmith ... 40

Old Dundee Lodge, No. 18... 7
Old King's Arms Lodge, No. 28 ... ... ... 14
Oxeland, Daniel, Founder ... 47

Parish Registers—St. Bennet Finck ... 16, 28
    Beddington ... ... 27
    French Protestant Church ... 19, 27
    Hammersmith ... ... 40
Past Masters, Ceremonies performed by them, 73, 74
Pepys, Samuel ... ... 8
Pike, James ... ... ... 63
Protestant French Church ... 19
Public Ledger ... ... 13
Pullen, T. H. (Clerk of St. Bennet Finck) ... ... 36

Queen Caroline ... ... 52

Radley's Hotel, Blackfriars... 68
Randall, Stephen ... ... 47
Rawlinson, Dr. Richard ... 8
Rawlinson, Sir Thomas ... 8
Rhodes (Angel Inn) ... ... 45
Ritual at Banquets ... ... 67
Rouse, William ... ... 67
Royal Arch Chapter Consecrated ... ... ... 67

Royal Exchange ... ... 10
Royal Inniskilling Dragoons 1
Royal Sussex Hotel, Hammersmith ... ... 42, 45
Rushworth (Angel Inn) ... 45

Sadler Henry, Grand Tyler, 6, 14, 63
St. Bennet Finck Church, 10, 20, 23, 24
St. Faith's Lodge ... ... 14
St. George's Lodge, No. 140 14
St. Luke's Lodge, No. 144 ... 14
St. Peter le Poer Church ... 16
St. Swithin's Alley ... ... 6
St. Swithin's Lane ... ... 37
Sala, George Augustus ... 31
Seager, H. W. ... ... 71
"Seasons," The ... ... 41
Secretaries of Lodge ... 84
Sich, John, P.M. ... ... 50
Simpson, Revd. R. J., P.G.C. 68
Sinclair, Archdeacon, P.G.C. 68
Slaughter, Mihill, P.A.G.D.C. Treasurer ... ... 71
Speer, Edward ... ... 53
Spread Eagle Court 6, 19, 28, 32, 36
Star and Garter, Kew Bridge 66
Suburbs, Extension of 9, 13, 14
Suspension Bridge, Hammersmith ... 42, 59, 61
Sussex, Duke of, Grand Master ... ... 41, 59
Sussex House ... ... 41
Swan and Rummer, Finch Lane ... ... ... 7
Sweeting's Rents, Royal Exchange ... ... 37

# INDEX

Ten-Broeke, Anthony ... 54
Thompson-Lawrence, P.M., P.G.D. ... ... ... 56
Thomson, Poet ... ... 41
Threadneedle Street  10, 36
Three Tun's Tavern ... 20
Treasurers of Lodge ... 83
Treasurer's Accounts  55, 56, 62
Tylers, Sword ... ... 60

Vaughan ... ... 13, 46, 47
Vestry Minutes (St. Bennet Finck) ... 16, 20, 23, 29

Warrant, Original ... ... 77
Warrant, Centenary ... ... 78
Waterland, Revd. Dr. ... 30
Watt, James, Engineer ... 28

Wedgwood, J. ... ... 10
West, Robert ... ... ... 55
Westminster and Keystone, No. 10 ... ... ... 14
Westminster Palace Hotel ... 68
Wharton, Duke of, Grand Master, 1723 ... ... 6
White Lion Tavern, Bishopsgate Street ... ... 13
White, John, P.M., Secretary 72
White, Wm. ... ... 36, 37
White, Wm. (Bell and Anchor Inn) ... ... ... 45
Wilkinson, R. ... ... 13
Wilson, John, Founder  14, 47
Wilson, S. Barton ... ... 63
Windsor Castle Inn, 13, 15, 42, 45, 53

Yean, Thomas ... ... 47
Younde, Thomas (Coffee House) ... ... ... 60

HARRINGTON & CO., PRINTERS,
93, GARRICK STREET, LONDON, W.C.

SUPPLEMENT

TO THE

HISTORY OF THE

"CAVEAC LODGE" No. 176.

BY

J. P. SIMPSON, P.M.

# SUPPLEMENT

TO THE

# HISTORY OF THE "CAVEAC LODGE." NO. 176.

IT will be in the recollection of the Brethren that one of the principal objects of my writing the History of the "Caveac Lodge" was to elucidate, if possible, the mystery which surrounded the name of the Lodge.

My theory as to this was that the Lodge at Hammersmith that received a Warrant in 1768 was but a continuation of an older City Lodge which ceased to meet at the Caveac Tavern, Spread Eagle Court, Threadneedle Street, just opposite the Broad Street entrance to the Stock Exchange, in the same year. The actual Buildings forming this Tavern afterwards became Lemann's Biscuit Manufactory, and were finally pulled down in 1849 in connection with the Royal Exchange Improvements Act.

Now, I should desire for a moment to call the attention of the Brethren to the names of five persons mentioned in my History, viz.:—Wm. Acton, of St. Margaret's, Lothbury, Painter, the last Master of the "Caveac Lodge" meeting at the old Caveac Tavern in 1768 (see page 7); John Caveac, the nephew of Bertrand Caveac, the Landlord of the Caveac Tavern who appears in the Parish Lists of 1769, and died 1781 (page 28); John Maddocks, Henry Adams and Vaughan, the first Master, and Wardens of the Caveac Lodge at Hammersmith (pages 46 & 47, and Warrant page 77). I give some account of the two former Brethren, and with regard to the three latter I mention on page 46 that I cannot trace their names in the Grand Lodge Records, but that possibly they were " experienced Masons who undertook to put the Brethren on the true Masonic line and rule, and then retired." I think the Brethren will agree with me that if the whole of the five names are found connected closely together we have discovered a final and conclusive link between the old Caveac Lodge in the City and the Lodge at Hammersmith.

This link has again been supplied by a happy accident, and through the kind instrumentality of my old friend Bro. Henry Sadler. When writing his interesting History of the Emulation Lodge, No. 21, he informed me that he had come across the name of John Caveac as a Member of that Lodge, and as he was described of Threadneedle Street, he presumed he was the same individual as mentioned in my book. On looking over the old Minute Books of the Emulation Lodge this proved to be the case, and the further important discovery was made that Wm. Acton of Lothbury was also a Member of the Emulation Lodge, and further that John Maddocks, Henry Adams, and John Vaughan were respectively Masters in the years 1767, 1768 and 1769.

> Wm. Acton was initiated in the Emulation Lodge 12th December, 1760.
> John Caveac of Threadneedle Street, proposed by John Lonesque, 13th July, 1772.
> John Maddocks of Castle Street, Laurence Lane, 12th August, 1763.
> Henry Adams 27th January, 1764.
> John Vaughan joined 25th December, 1764.

I think without doubt what happened was that Wm. Acton, finding he could not assist his old Lodge at Hammersmith, asked three prominent Members of his Mother Lodge, Brothers Maddocks, Adams and Vaughan, experienced Craftsmen, to put the Brethren at Hammersmith on the true Masonic line and rule, as I conjectured in my History, and thus to give them a good send off. This they very kindly consented to do, and hence probably the peculiar wording of the Warrant: "And do further at their said Petition, and of the great trust and confidence reposed in every of the said above-named Three Brethren Do hereby appoint John Maddocks to be Master, Henry Adams Senior Warden, and        Vaughan Junior Warden for opening the said Lodge, and for such further time only as shall be thought proper by the Brethren thereof." It is somewhat late after the lapse of 138 years to return thanks for this kindly and fraternal action, but I think a decided debt of gratitude is due by us to the Emulation Lodge, No. 21.

I should like also to point out that in my History I omitted to mention that the Lodge meeting at the Caveac Tavern originally met at the Blossoms Inn, Laurence Lane, on the 12th December, 1736; Buffaloes Head, Finch Lane, 1744; Fountain, Bartholomew Lane, 1745; and the Caveac Tavern, 1755 to 1768.

A short extract from my Paper, "Old City Taverns and Masonry," in the Quattuor Coronati Transactions may be of interest. It relates to the Blossoms Inn, the first home of the Lodge.

"A little further east in Lawrence Lane once stood
"'THE BLOSSOMS INN,' (*Plate No. XII*) one of the most
"ancient in the City. Stow refers to it as 'among many
"fair houses there is one large Inn for the receipt of
"Travellers called Blossoms Inn, but corruptly Bossums
"Inn, and hath a sign, St. Lawrence the Deacon, in a
"border of blossoms or flowers.' The legend of St.
"Lawrence is that he was martyred by being roasted
"alive on a gridiron, and that flowers sprang up on the
"spot. In the reign of Henry VIII, 1522, the Emperer
"Charles V visited England, and an enquiry was held as
"to the accommodation of certain Inns for housing his

"retinue. 'The Blossoms' is put down as having '20 beddes and stabling for 60 horses' (Rutland Papers, Camden Society). Ben Jonson also refers to it in his Masque of Christmas:—

"But now comes Tom of Blossoms Inn
"And he presenteth misrule."

"At this Inn a Master's Lodge (the Caveac) met as early as 1736, the Royal Kent Lodge of Antiquity No. 20 in 1741, and the Jordan Lodge No. 201 as late as 1831. Soon after this date it was pulled down, but the name is still retained in Blossoms Yard, the receiving office of the Great Eastern Railway."

SOME FURTHER EXTRACTS FROM THE MINUTES OF GRAND LODGE AND "MALCOLM'S ANECDOTES OF LONDON MANNERS IN THE 18TH CENTURY" THROW SOME FURTHER LIGHT ON THE LODGE HISTORY.

From GRAND LODGE MINUTES, QUARTERLY COMMUNICATION, 29th October, 1765.
Concerning Warrant Caveac Lodge. Finch Lane. Two of the Brethren attending.

"The Master of the CAVEAC LODGE was for surrendering the Constitutions. A Member of the said LODGE approved it. ORDERED that the Brethren be summoned to the next C.C."

At a Meeting of the Charity Committee for the disposal of the GENERAL CHARITY at the HORN TAVERN in Fleet Street, January 22nd, 1766.

"The complaint of several Brethren of the Caveac Lodge Finch Lane preferred against the Master, and other Brethren of the said LODGE and referred by the last Quarterly Communication to this Committee of Charity setting forth that the said LODGE had "been regularly dissolved notwithstanding which the "Master and Wardens still continued to hold the said "LODGE as usual, and praying that the Dissolution "of the said Lodge might be confirmed was heard, and "duly considered. RESOLVED UNANIMOUSLY "that the said pretended dissolution of the LODGE "was illegal, and therefore that the said LODGE ought "still to subsist, and recommended Harmony to the "Brethren for the future, and a choice of new Officers "of the LODGE next lodge night."

The above extracts show beyond doubt that the name "Caveac Lodge" was applied to the Lodge meeting at the Old Tavern at the corner of Finch Lane and Threadneedle Street, and several years before the Warrant was granted in 1768 for the Lodge at Hammersmith.

EXTRACT FROM MALCOLM'S ANECDOTES OF LONDON MANNERS OF 18TH CENTURY. Vol. 1, page 279.

"Near the Exchange are two very good French "Eating Houses, the one the Sign of Pontack a President "of the Parliament of Bordeaux from whose name the "best French Clarets are called, and where you can "bespeak a Dinner from 4/- or 5/- a head to a guinea "or what sum you please. The other is CAVEACK'S "where there is a constant Ordinary as abroad for all "comers without distinction, and at a very reasonable "price."

Lightning Source UK Ltd.
Milton Keynes UK
UKHW040645120220
358601UK00002B/404